One thing is for sure: you'll likely never see loyalty the same way after reading this book. So fasten your seat belt, sit back and enjoy a ride that brings loyalty to life.

Martin Lindstrom, *New York Times* bestselling author and business transformation expert

This book is a must-read for executives in the retail space and also has insightful lessons for those in the airline and hotel industries. No matter how your company is positioned in the retail marketplace, properly designed and executed loyalty programmes deliver meaningful value creation.

David Adams, former chief financial officer, Aimia/Nectar

In a world of sameness, with retailers in need of customer loyalty more than ever before, this book opens the door to proven ways to engage shoppers and build enduring customer relationships. Essential reading.

Dr Kjell A Nordström, bestselling author and economist

Richard Beattie is one of the pioneers in loyalty and his expertise has assisted well-known food retailers across the globe. Bringing Loyalty to Life *is a hands-on guide to understanding the power of loyalty at retail and implementing world-class programmes.*

Gary Hawkins, CEO and founder, Center for Advancing Retail & Technology

Richard has written a good book about 'boots on the ground' retailing. Historically in 20th century business the desk farthest away from the front door was where the person in charge sat. Loyalty marketing is about changing that paradigm.

Paco Underhill, bestselling author and founder, Envirosell Global

Insightful and practical, Richard Beattie's book offers valuable lessons and actionable advice on creating successful customer loyalty programmes. A must-read for any marketing and retail professional looking to stay ahead in an ever-changing industry.

Kenny Chien, CEO, Cherrypicks

To E D Wallace

His legacy lives on

BRINGING LOYALTY TO LIFE

How to earn, build and leverage
enduring customer loyalty

RICHARD BEATTIE

Bringing Loyalty to Life

ISBN 978-1-915483–20–1 (hardback)

eISBN 978-1-915483–22-5

Published in 2023 by Right Book Press

A CIP record of this book is available from the British Library.

CONTENTS

FOREWORD

by Martin Lindstrom

After recently spending months in Europe for business, I was happy to finally be heading back home to Sydney. It was on this trip that I experienced loyalty on a level I had never witnessed. Taking my seat aboard a Singapore Airlines flight, I noticed an envelope neatly placed atop the seat's unfolded tray table. 'Welcome Home' the lettering on the envelope read. Inside it I found a selection of ten different Australian newspapers accompanied by a memo beaming with warm sentiment: 'We know you've been away from home for nearly a month. It's hard keeping track of what's happening on the other side of the world – so we thought we would help you. Here's a little selection of all the breaking news that's happened over the past 4 weeks. Welcome home.'

I've been loyal to Singapore Airlines for 24 years.

Or have I? Of my last six flights, three were with Emirates, two were with Swiss International, and one – yes, only one – was with Singapore Airlines. The memo says that I'm loyal, the system says I'm loyal, I'm even saying to the world 'I'm loyal'. But am I really?

My dad worked at two different companies throughout his entire life. An average kid growing up today and easing into the workforce will not only be 'loyal' to more than 15 different jobs, but each of their jobs will also represent completely different trades, skills and industries. The changing definition of loyalty is visible everywhere. One hardcore Chanel fan once disclosed to me that she only wears Chanel 'on the outside' – underneath, she dons whatever is cheapest. Fire up

Spotify and begin listening to whatever the algorithm recommends – and I bet you'll struggle to tell me who's singing. Yes, from time to time you do hear your favourite artists – but how often?

Does the concept of loyalty even exist in today's world? Let's look at the institution of marriage. Certain marriage vows include the declaration 'until death do us part'. In reality, however, the average American is married at least twice in their lifetime. And if you're Elizabeth Taylor, you've been married eight times. Turning to music, typical listeners on average make it through only two thirds of their favourite songs before moving on. What about food? During the pandemic, one third of Americans switched supermarkets. As you can see, loyalty is undergoing a profound disruption.

With that in mind, I reached out to three sources to try to understand what the universal – and may I add, permanent – truth of loyalty would be to gain a perspective of what loyalty always will be.

'Loyalty is contextual,' Ana Brant, the head of customer experience at Wynn Las Vegas, told me. 'There is no such thing as a single-minded loyalty format anymore. We may have the most loyal guests at our casinos – tied in via the most generous loyalty programs – yet a 'party of the year' taking place down the road from us at one of our competitors, attended by our customers' best friends, means they'll move it all away from us in a heartbeat.' It's all about context – something few loyalty programs really understand or take into consideration.

'Loyalty is a two-way street,' Edward Mady, former head of the iconic Beverly Hills Hotel and Bel Air in Los Angeles – and hotelier of the year – told me. There must be an 'investment' taking place both ways; it cannot be just one party making such an investment. However, once a two-way investment takes place, loyalty becomes a long-term play.

Another consideration with respect to how the concept of loyalty has been upended is artificial intelligence (AI). What role will AI play in its construction? Will loyalty become a thing of the past, or will technological innovations shift the sands to help loyalty to strengthen and grow?

I couldn't think of anyone better to ask than ChatGPT:

Yes, loyalty can still exist in a world where artificial intelligence (AI) is embedded into everything we do, including ChatGPT. Loyalty is a human characteristic that involves feelings of allegiance, commitment, and devotion to a person, organization, or cause. Although I can automate many tasks it and decision-making processes, it cannot replace the emotions and connections that humans have with each other and the things they are loyal to.

In fact, AI can even enhance loyalty by helping businesses and organizations better understand their customers' preferences and needs. By using data analytics and machine learning algorithms, AI can personalize and improve customer experiences, leading to greater loyalty.

However, it's important to note that AI technology and its impact on loyalty is still a relatively new and evolving field. As AI technology continues to advance, it's possible that new ethical and social issues may arise that could impact loyalty in unforeseen ways.

The core of what loyalty is will remain intact, but the way it is built, maintained and strengthened will evolve. To survive, loyalty must become more contextual, simultaneously flow in two directions and, most importantly, dial up the human aspect and exhibit vulner-abilities, transparency and empathy.

And that's just the beginning, as you'll soon discover. In this book, Richard Beattie takes you through an insightful and deep dive into the world of loyalty. For instance, who would have thought that loyalty programs were introduced more than 400 years ago by Queen Mary and William of Orange? And that the concept of coupons was first introduced and found in soap packages in 1850? And that, upon American Airlines' unveiling of the world's first frequent flyer program, the company was challenged by commentators who said that giving people free flights made no sense whatsoever.

Since then, the term 'loyalty' and the methods used to challenge the discipline have evolved a hundred times over. In the following chapters, Beattie takes readers through a fascinating journey as he opens the door to the engine room. Few have experienced, witnessed and implemented as many initiatives as Beattie and his team at TCC. You'll also learn about the new kids on the block and how they are likely to fundamentally change how we deal with loyalty. The roles that AI, big data and gaming play are likely to change. The ever-changing roles of retailers, ecommerce and even the metaverse will too. If you think you knew it all, you've got the right book in your hands.

Bringing Loyalty to Life will make your head spin – but in a good way. Loyalty has, on the one hand, become an art form or a philosophy, while on the other hand, it has tapped into sophisticated big data, algorithms and augmented reality (AR). It is a fine balance, ensuring that the human side stays intact while still scalable. Handling this balancing act, you'll come across landmines that few would ever imagine – well, with the exception of Beattie. He identifies the obstacles for you. And this book captures the essence of what it takes to stay impactful in an ever-oversaturated world.

One thing is for sure: you'll likely never see loyalty the same way again after having read this book. So, fasten your seat belt, sit back and enjoy a ride that helps bring loyalty to life.

Martin Lindstrom is one of the world's leading brand, culture, and transformation experts, according to the Wall Street Journal. *For ten years running he has been featured as a top business thinker by the prestigious Thinkers50 list and* TIME *magazine has named Lindstrom one of the 'World's 100 Most Influential People'. Lindstrom's books include eight* New York Times *and* Wall Street Journal *bestsellers, including* Buyology *and* Small Data, *which have been translated into 60 languages.*

ACKNOWLEDGEMENTS

This book couldn't have happened without the help and support of a number of people and our company's story is built on the efforts of many more.

I'm now faced with the dilemma of thanking a few people who helped with the book and the wider group of people who helped us to build the company.

So please let me thank you all for making this book come alive and more importantly in making TCC such a success.

Of course, I must thank Teena Lyons (see overleaf) who listened patiently over the many months, gave us great counsel and wove this rambling narrative into a finished manuscript.

Thanks to my co-founders Una Byrne and Gordon Cooper, who helped me tell our story.

Sue Richardson, Beverley Glick, Paul East and Andrew Chapman at The Right Book Company guided us through the minefield that is book publishing, working alongside Rob Chappelhow in a coordinating role.

And finally, I want to thank our many loyal clients and their shoppers, who gave us their business right back then in our humble beginnings and still do today, because I'm afraid that otherwise this would have been a rather slim edition!

Likewise, our many loyal suppliers and brand partners who've stayed with us over these past 30 years.

Thank you all.

Richard Beattie
Hong Kong, May 2023

Teena Lyons

Teena Lyons spent the early part of her career as a financial and consumer affairs journalist. She spent seven years as retail correspondent at the *Mail on Sunday*, breaking a number of high-profile news stories and regularly interviewing the most important business leaders in the sector. She also wrote for a number of other national newspapers including *The Daily Telegraph*, *The Guardian* and *The Sunday Times*, as well as contributing to a range of consumer and trade press magazine titles, including *Cosmopolitan*, *Woman* and *The Grocer*. Since 2006 she has been an author and ghostwriter, specialising in business books and biographies.

INTRODUCTION

When I visited an old friend in Melbourne, Australia recently, he recounted the story about our first holiday to Cornwall, in south-west England, shortly after we'd both turned 16. We couldn't afford hotels and wondered where we were going to sleep. Then he had a bright idea. He said, 'My mum's got these books of Green Shield Stamps,' so we went to his house, grabbed them and went to redeem them for a two-person tent. (For those readers who are too young to remember, Green Shield Stamps were a popular British sales promotion scheme founded in 1958 that rewarded shoppers with stamps that could be used to redeem gifts from a catalogue or affiliated retailers.) I'll never forget that tent – it's a treasured memory, just like the memories shared by many people who are still eating off the dinnerware or using the luggage that they were gifted in a rewards programme 10, 20 years ago. And it proves that what we do in the loyalty business is deeply rooted in the human psyche.

Let me share another true story about how powerful loyalty can be. There were two major grocery chains, both operating in the top five in their home country. Store A, a privately run business, had been trading for a century or more and had built up a strong following among its customers. It had a reputation for being solid and dependable, a place you could always rely on for good quality goods and services. Store B had a similar provenance in terms of age, except it was a cooperative, jointly owned and run by the members. Its reputation was built on keen pricing and the fact that everyone could count on a share of the profits.

When The Continuity Company (now TCC) launched more than 30 years ago, we were working hard to expand our client base. We'd done a little work with Store A and Store B, so when a potential international customer said they'd be coming over to chat to us, we decided to take them on a tour of each shop. First we took them around a shop in the Store A chain and followed up with a visit to one of Store B's shops. Our keen-eyed guests noticed that there were gaps in the shelves in both stores.

'Isn't this lack of stock a problem for your customers?' one of our guests asked the Store B manager who'd been showing us around. 'We saw the same issue at the other store.'

The Store B manager smiled and shrugged his shoulders.

'In our shop, yes, it is a big problem,' he said. 'Our customers don't hesitate to complain that we've let them down and tell us we need to get our house in order.'

There was, he sighed, a very different reaction when customers saw Store A had sold out of their favourite products.

'Their customers are so loyal to the brand, they see no wrong there. When they see an empty shelf, they blame themselves for getting there too late.'

And that, in a nutshell, is what loyalty can achieve. However, things have changed a lot since then. There are few brands that can count on such unerring, unconditional loyalty; brands that are so highly regarded that no one ever seems to think ill of them, even if they get something wrong. You could perhaps put Apple or Amazon in this category but after that might struggle to name brands that are equally invincible. This means that other brands need to work at creating loyalty to reap the benefits that go with that allegiance.

A colleague reminded me of the story of Store A and Store B during what was supposed to be a flying visit to our UK office in early 2020 but which turned into a lengthy stay thanks to the pandemic.

I was there to discuss preparations for the celebration of our 30th anniversary. It was a milestone moment and, as we looked back, we found that some of the statistics we'd been compiling about the company were staggering. We calculated that, during our three decades in business, we'd launched more than 8,000 loyalty solutions and engaged with more than one billion shoppers. To achieve this, we'd worked with 250 retailers across 70 countries giving away collections of everything from Barbie dolls to Hot Wheels to MasterChef bakeware. Sometimes, the sheer scale of the campaigns we've been involved in has been breathtaking. When the Teenage Mutant Hero Turtle craze was at its height in the 1990s, we minted more than 100 million metal coins celebrating the franchise in the 'official medal collection' for a newspaper promotion. Every single medal was snapped up. As we reflected on some of the stories behind these numbers, the idea emerged of writing a book to share what we've learned over the years. After all, we have a great deal of valuable experience that retailers may find useful.

While we've only ever had one simple goal – changing shopper behaviour by increasing store visits and growing average basket size – strategies have inevitably changed and developed over time. The way we shop has changed immeasurably over the past few generations. When I was young, no one would consider going anywhere other than the village butcher for their meat and the baker for their bread. I still recall how that changed almost overnight when an Asda supermarket opened nearby. That unquestioning loyalty to independent stores didn't vanish overnight but it definitely started the inexorable decline. It's no coincidence that loyalty has diminished at the same rate as chain stores have continued to grow in size and popularity around the globe. With the days of unconditional loyalty now firmly in the past, retailers have had to work increasingly hard to ensure customers have a real sense of attachment to a given store.

The modern loyalty challenge has been compounded by the growth of digital. The global ecommerce market is expected to top $5.55 trillion in 2022. According to Shopify (Keenan 2022), a percentage of total retail sales, online accounts for 21 per cent, up from 18 per cent in 2020. What's more, consumers can buy goods from virtually anywhere in the world. The days when my local butcher 'only' had to contend with competition from the new Asda superstore are long gone. It's not just small independents either. All shops, however large, face competition from all sides. To compete, bricks and mortar retailers need to give shoppers a compelling reason to visit a physical store and they need to make sure they make the effort to shop the whole store. A well thought through loyalty programme should be at the core of this strategy.

Retail is not the only landscape that has changed immeasurably. The world in which we operate has changed markedly too. There is now, quite rightly, much more interest in the bigger picture, whether it's climate change, sustainability or how we live and support one another within our communities. According to TCC figures, the vast majority of consumers (88 per cent) want retailers to step up to help them make a difference. They expect them to care about people and the planet. Like every business, we've had to give some thought to our own role in this, as we are a cog in this complex world. We've had to consider how we deliver our core purpose – impactful loyalty programmes that build deeper relationships with shoppers – while also still being a force for good. Being a force for good means that, when we design our loyalty campaigns, everyone wins: customers, retailers, suppliers, communities and the planet. It's just as important to be purposeful as profitable, creating campaigns that increase sales, raise awareness and drive loyalty forward.

It's just as important to be purposeful as profitable, creating campaigns that increase sales, raise awareness and drive loyalty forward.

We've moved with the times and, over the past few years, we've made huge strides towards this goal, leading the way with purpose-built campaigns focusing on sustainability, community and a brighter future for all. In the two-year period before writing this book, we've moved from a position where none of our rewards had a significant focus on sustainability to one where 30 per cent of our rewards are fully sustainable. This is just the beginning, though, and we're constantly looking at our supply chain to see where we can do better. Later on in this book, you'll find details of all the different areas in which we're making significant adjustments to change and focus on what really matters and of the accreditations we've already achieved. We're also working closely with retailers to design campaigns that actively focus on measures to help their shoppers' lives and improve the communities in which they live. We've already seen ample evidence that carefully targeted campaigns can make a disproportional impact on people's lives. All of this, of course, runs alongside promotions that deliver 3 or 4 per cent sales increases to retailers.

There are many more changes on the horizon. As I write, we're entering a period of high inflation and recession, even stagflation. Supply chains are under pressure and, with energy costs soaring, some households face the impossible choice between heating and eating. All of this will impact the retail sector, further fuelling the shift towards discounters. Retailers are focused on what they can do to make their customers' lives a little easier and rewards programmes should be a part of this endeavour.

While things are moving forward at a pace, I also believe there are lessons to be learned from the past. Much of what we do today has been shaped by historic loyalty campaigns and we set great store in the knowledge we've gained in our 30 years. Our company name, for example, contains a respectful nod to one of the origins of collecting in the retail context. The term 'continuity' originates from the TV and film business. According to dictionary.com, a continuity person takes care of 'the maintenance of continuous action and self-consistent detail in the various scenes or broadcast'. Or, to put it in more user-friendly terms, they are the individual who looks for mistakes in shoots. If, say, there's a half-full glass on the table and a pair of shoes at the door, they make sure the items are in the exact same place for each subsequent shot.

Over time, continuity grew to become the term to indicate an ongoing gift promotion that attracts and builds customer loyalty – the idea being that if anyone collects a piece of glassware, cutlery or ceramics, it's a little pointless stopping at only one piece. The entire purpose of a continuity programme is based on encouraging people to return again and again, and it works so well because so many of us have a compulsion to collect. Whether it's stamps, Hello Kitty merchandise or football cards, collecting gives us an enormous sense of pride in our achievements.

My own career in continuity programmes began when I was persuaded to quit a good and secure job with News Corp in Australia to join an American company called Wallace International. The person who persuaded me that it was a good idea was Dan Wallace. I have little doubt that the epithet 'larger than life' was coined for Dan. He was a big man with an even bigger personality. (He was later celebrated in the 2003 film Big Fish, staring Ewan McGregor and Albert Finney and based on the book written by Dan's son Daniel Wallace Junior.) When Dan Wallace was enthusiastic about something it was hard to ignore. It so happened that he was extremely enthusiastic about what could be achieved by giving away kitchen equipment and homeware to encourage shoppers to visit the same store week after week. Thanks to promotions organised by Wallace International, every time people visited their local grocery store, they gained a reward. It might be a dinner plate one week, a matching bowl the next. Over time, it eventually built up to become a complete matching dinner service.

My new role involved looking after Wallace International's interests outside the US and Canada. Despite small beginnings working out of my flat in Elizabeth Bay in eastern Sydney, my hunch that it would work out OK was quickly proved right. In the interests of full disclosure, I should point out that I had a rather lucky (or perhaps quite cheeky) early break. While still contracted to News Corp I'd secured an appointment to speak to the CEO of the Coles supermarket chain about a A$50 million piece of business. By the date of the appointment, I'd already resigned. I still went to see the Coles CEO and delivered a compelling presentation about partworks and continuity marketing. It wasn't until the end that I slipped in the additional yet essential piece of information that I was now representing Wallace International, not News Corp. I was pretty nervous about the CEO's reaction but he didn't bat an eyelid.

This was a huge milestone in my continuity career and led on to more than A$500 million of business during my 12 years with Coles. The supermarket used all the principal reward categories over the years, from cookware and luggage to plush animals. After starting out by taking charge of our interests in Australia, New Zealand and South Africa, I subsequently took the lead in the UK and the rest of Europe.

In 1991, I decided to go it alone and launch The Continuity Company. My involvement with Wallace International had reached a natural ending. Dan Wallace's son had decided that he didn't want to inherit the business when the time came, so Wallace International was put up for sale. The process was difficult, protracted and contentious, and while I'd briefly toyed with buying the business myself, it seemed better to start from scratch. This decision was proved right when Wallace International collapsed into receivership in August 1991 under a mountain of debt (Casemine 2000). It was revived and relaunched but never really recovered.

Like most new small businesses, my first challenge was raising the money to get started. It soon emerged that the banks had no appetite for a firm offering loyalty programmes, so everything we did needed to be funded organically or out of my own pocket. TCC began with a similar goal to Wallace International: to bring about stronger connections between retailers and customers. And, just like Wallace International, we started off small. This time, rather than operating out of an apartment in Elizabeth Bay, we set up shop in my flat in Airlie Gardens in London's Kensington. As well as working within the UK, we made Italy our first international market and planned to expand into other countries we knew well, including Australia, France, Holland and Hong Kong.

Many of our early pitches were very successful. Our first campaigns were with the Italian chains Generale Supermercati (now Carrefour) and PAM Supermercati, giving away collections of Pyrex and Guzzini bakeware. In our first year, despite a number of challenges, we got off to a flying start, achieving a turnover equivalent to €34 million in guilders. (Our headquarters were in the Netherlands, which still took the currency until 2002, when it switched to the euro.) In a short space of time, up to 20 people filled the Airlie Gardens flat and it was somewhat cosy to say the least. Some of the other team members around the world also hosted countless others in their own apartments.

What we quickly came to realise was that, even though continuity programmes had been around for some years, if we were to grow the business further there was still a job to be done to convince many retailers. We often had to explain that the success of a loyalty promotion is built on the excitement shoppers experience when receiving a succession of free rewards. Even if it was a nominal amount, if customers were asked to contribute towards rewards, it wouldn't be anywhere near as powerful.

It wasn't just a case of convincing clients, either. Campaign by campaign, new territory by new territory, we learned a lot too. Some lessons are fairly obvious. The homemaker is still the main target for rewards of kitchen goods anywhere in the world. They have almost identical triggers, too: they enjoy and value being given something for free. We also found that some promotions are ubiquitous and will work anywhere in the world while others won't always find a good home in every location. A cutlery promotion wouldn't create much excitement in Japan, for example, where chopsticks are more frequently used. It therefore makes sense to adapt locally where applicable. Likewise, some brands carry significant cachet in certain locations but are viewed with indifference elsewhere. Customers in Italy value Alessi and Guzzini, whereas in Germany, Fissler is the cookware brand. Likewise, nowadays Italian supermarkets wouldn't dream of running a promotion unless sustainability was a major factor in the rewards range on offer. Meanwhile, some Asian countries prioritise rewards with a social impact.

One of the most satisfying of all the lessons we learned was that when we got it right, the response could be astonishing. This was brought home to us during one of our earliest cookware promotions in Hong Kong. Our collection had proved to be so collectable that there were no items left. This was exacerbated by the fact that a ship with a container of rewards on board had capsized. When a lorry finally arrived with a restock, it was besieged by shoppers. Fights began to break out and the police had to be called in to control the crowds. The first we knew about it was via a somewhat frantic call from one of our team, a rather dour Scotsman. His house was located on the hill above one of the supermarkets hosting the promotion, so he had a grandstand view. After he told us what was going on, we asked him to go down and appease the crowds. His immediate response was that he wasn't going to risk going down there, except the wording was not quite as polite as that! We had to get the local radio station involved to reassure everyone that extra stock was being rushed to Hong Kong at that very moment. The radio interview helped but there was an unintended downside. The interviewer couldn't get over the fact that there had been near riots over free cookware and wanted to know everything about the promotion. Their extended report about the range on offer was so glowing it earned the (already oversubscribed) retailer even more collectors – including the radio interviewer.

Even though we've learned so much over the years, we're still learning all the time. It's crucial that we keep listening to what customers want and the values they find important. Whenever I speak with retailers to make sure we're still on track and pursuing strategies that appeal, I'm often reminded of a survey I read in Good Housekeeping magazine around 30 years ago, around the time of The Continuity Company's launch. The magazine had carried out an interesting exercise. It had asked the same question to a number of retail chief executives about what they thought customers most wanted. The differences in the responses were so stark as to be truly remarkable. The list offered by the retail bosses covered such things as shorter queuing times at the checkout, a larger range of products and keener prices. But customers? Well, their responses were eclectic to say the least. One of the biggest bugbears highlighted by shoppers was children standing up in trolleys. Many cited concerns that the youngsters would fall and injure themselves. Mind you, they could simply have been irritated by them, certainly if the next response was anything to go by. Shoppers also vocalised a certain amount of impatience and frustration with elderly people getting in their way. The final point, which was enough to get shoppers to go elsewhere, was a lack of toilets. It was clear that the two sides, retailers and customers, were worlds apart in terms of what they thought mattered.

The retail landscape is constantly changing. To keep the attention of shoppers and make sure they come back time and again, we need to understand what moves them. While there are mountains of data to help us, there's little substitute for experience. Hence the reason for this book. After 30 years in the business during which we've been involved in some of the world's most high-profile loyalty schemes, we'd like to think we understand a lot about the behavioural aspects of loyalty. Ultimately, each individual is more than just data and we don't all fit into neat little boxes. This book outlines the lessons we've learned along the way, what works, what doesn't and what the future holds for loyalty. We hope you enjoy our insights and find them useful in your business.

1 LESSONS FROM LOYALTY'S PAST (AND PRESENT)

1. Keep customer interest alive (with thanks to B T Babbit)

History tells us that gifts were being given as rewards for loyalty more than 400 years ago. One of the first recorded examples can be found during the reign of Queen Mary and William of Orange (1689–1702). According to a 1994 study (Castaldo & Mauri), tea bowls were gifted to buyers of the then newly popular drink of tea, which was imported via tea chests. The goal then was the same as it is now: to influence purchasers.

Promotional techniques have, not surprisingly, changed a lot in the intervening years. However, as so often happens, there are some interesting lessons from the past that influence where we are now and where we may go in the future. For this reason, I'll begin this book with a recap of what we've learned from some of the changing trends before going into a little more detail about the types of loyalty you might encounter today.

Over time, loyalty promotions have gradually developed to become more complex and sophisticated, offering a greater range and choice of rewards. From the beginning, this trend has been driven by customer demand. We can see a great example of this in the progression of one of the earliest known American loyalty schemes.

The story began in 1850, when B T Babbit, a soap manufacturer, launched a laundry soap. Until that point, it was the norm for grocers to slice soap into long strips at the point of purchase. Babbit decided that a more efficient approach would be to pre-package the soap in ready-made slices and present them wrapped in a sheet of paper. Being a commercially minded fellow, he made sure that the paper bore his name. To begin with, the women who purchased his soap were utterly unmoved. The clear message was that they wanted to buy soap but not paper. In their view, the paper added no value whatsoever – and it was a fair point. At this time no one had even considered linking the idea of convenience with the shopping experience. Babbit, however, was still convinced he was onto something and began printing coupons on the paper packaging. If a customer collected 25 of these coupons, they could exchange them for the gift of a coloured lithograph. Now, this was more like it and shoppers responded positively to the concept. So much so, in fact, that rival soap manufacturers quickly followed suit with their own coupons. Over time, they too developed the idea, offering figurines as well as lithographs in exchange for a number of coupons. Again, this was well received: demand became so great that the ante was upped once again and figurines began to be included in each pack of soap.

Rewards needed to be something everyone valued but there also needed to be regular changes to sustain that interest.

Babbit realised that it was crucial to keep customer interest alive. Rewards needed to be something everyone valued but there also needed to be regular changes to sustain that interest, especially with rival soap makers flooding the market with gifts. Babbit's next innovation was to allow the customer to choose their gift.

He produced a catalogue offering everything from toothbrushes and watches to corsets. Again, the response was positive. This time, it wasn't just other soap makers that saw the possibilities behind the idea. Tobacco, coffee, tea and milk manufacturers also started introducing coupons for their wares. The resulting coupon collecting fervour spawned an entirely new hobby for American consumers: cashing in coupons. Designated premium distribution centres popped up and were frequented by eager collectors who treated them like gift shops. The joy being, of course, that everything in that shop was 'free' in exchange for their coupons. With enough coupons, the gifts could be pretty substantial too.

Another forerunner to loyalty as we know it today is the concept of partworks. Partworks is a term that describes a series of booklets and magazines that are released by newsagents on a weekly basis, covering subjects from health to myths and magic, the history of the Second World War and great composers. Households would collect parts in the series week by week, building them up into an encyclopaedic collection that comprehensively covered the entire subject.

The idea goes back to 1875, when an American company called Funk & Wagnalls published religious texts as partworks, encouraging worshippers to build their own collections. These texts were widely available from supermarkets, where shoppers were always tempted in with the offer of the first in the series for free, with subsequent issues sold at 99 cents. Over time, the partworks would build into a set of 28 or 30 books, which could be stored in a gold-embossed volume that would frequently take pride of place on bookshelves up and down the land. What was particularly special about these partworks was the high-quality finish. Collectors would always be enthralled by the fantastic presentation, for which they only paid a matter of dollars week by week.

2. Attract new customers while rewarding existing ones

One of the most important shifts in collecting was when promotions became available to all consumers, not just those who already frequented a particular store on a regular basis. This broader outlook meant the reward, or gift, needed to be advertised to the outside world. The first evidence of this thinking dates back to Italy in the 1930s. Buitoni-Perugina, a large Italian food company, sponsored The Four Musketeers, a popular comedic radio series loosely based on The Three Musketeers by French author Alexandre Dumas. The link with the radio series, to promote its figurine collection sticker books of characters in the series, was the first ever loyalty programme on a national scale and capitalised on the popular Italian hobby of collecting figurines. Customers who completed sets of 100 figurines could choose a gift from one of Buitoni-Perugina's products such as a box of chocolates, Perugina candles or Buitoni pastas. If they chose to keep collecting, they could redeem them for higher-value rewards featured in a premium catalogue. Those rewards, which required thousands of figurines to redeem, ranged from radios, Olivetti typewriters and Bianchi bicycles to the top prize of a Fiat 500 car. (The Fiat 500 made its debut in 1936 and was much coveted throughout Italy.) While interest in the promotion was already high, thanks to the popularity of the radio show, Buitoni-Perugina also made a lot of additional noise via records featuring recordings of the show, leaflets and at various specially convened events.

This broader outlook meant the reward, or gift, needed to be advertised to the outside world.

3. Accurate planning and forecasting are crucial

The success of the Buitoni-Perugina promotion also highlighted another important lesson about rewards-based promotions: accurate planning and forecasting are crucial. A delay in the delivery of sketches by Angelo Bioletto, the designer of the series of figurines, led to a severe shortage of one particular figurine, a character called Ferocious Saladin. This rarity instantly made Ferocious Saladin much sought after but, where there's demand, there are often unscrupulous characters ready to step in to take advantage of it. In fact, so lucrative was the proposition that many of Italy's finest banknote counterfeiters switched to a new career for a while, producing counterfeit Ferocious Saladins. In the ensuing chaos, with the police being forced to intervene, the Italian Ministry of Corporations introduced a law requiring businesses such as Buitoni-Perugina to print the same number of copies of every gift in future promotions. Many other countries followed suit, enacting a series of standards for gifts and rewards.

Since this time there have been a few more bumps in the road. Indisputably, Hoover must be in the running to win the crown for one of the most infamous loyalty disasters. Their case was as much to do with poor planning as a lack of strict controls. The story unfolded in the early 1990s, when some bright spark came up with a compelling offer: free flights for any customer that spent more than £100 on a vacuum cleaner. Even though Hoover took care to make the redemption process extremely complicated, it didn't take long before tens of thousands of bright (and determined) customers worked out that the £100 purchase price of a Hoover vacuum cleaner was a lot, lot cheaper than the cost of a £600 flight to the US. Word of the unbelievable offer quickly spread and sales of Hoovers soared. Some of the thousands that bought Hoover products didn't even bother collecting them from the store; they were only in it for the free flight. The promotion was a disaster, leading to legal action, a host of senior executives losing their jobs and the loss of the business's royal warrant. It's now considered to be the worst sales promotion in history (Crockett 2019).

Other parties play an influential role too, helping to steer the decision to shop at a particular store or buy a specific item.

4. Think beyond the purchaser

For many years, rewards were designed to appeal solely to the person who bought and paid for the goods connected to the promotion. Then it emerged that other parties play an influential role too, helping to steer the decision to shop at a particular store or buy a specific item. The input could come from other family members, particularly children, but close friends could be an influence too. This realisation played a part in the extended list of rewards presented in catalogues by Buitoni-Perugina and other retailers around the world. To begin with, the gifts were purely aimed at women, who used to take on the bulk of the shopping tasks. This was subsequently extended to men and then, in 1963, Mira Lanza, another Italian retailer, leveraged the power of children. Just over a decade earlier, the manufacturer of laundry detergents had launched a catalogue-style points collection programme to fight back against the growing popularity of two rival detergents, Olà and Omo. To begin with, the gifts on offer in Mira Lanza's catalogues were designed to appeal to housewives, giving away items such as china, blankets and textiles in return for tokens. Realising that mums were susceptible to pester power, a charming but hapless chick called Calimero was created, along with a series of Adventures of Calimero figurines that were given away free at Mira Lanza cash tills. Children were invited to collect the figurines to reconstruct the same stories they saw in an Italian TV production called Carosello, which starred Calimero. Indeed, it was this series which led to the term 'soap operas' being coined, referencing the role the detergent manufacturer had played in creating TV shows which engaged the whole family. After this, loyalty programmes began to have a far more family-friendly focus.

5. Loyalty programmes can be powerful drivers of growth

Before it adopted its family-focused loyalty campaign, Mira Lanza had been in a precarious financial position. Indeed, it was close to bankruptcy and had initially been reticent about adopting it because of the cost involved in promotion. But going ahead was the right choice: between 1957 and 1970, the company was the consistent leader in the detergent market with a 25 per cent market share. The increased sales were crucial in helping the firm overcome its earlier difficulties.

Another campaign during the same period, this time in the UK, was credited by Tesco as being one of its 'most powerful drivers of growth' (Humby et al 2003). The retailer had embraced the Green Shield Stamps scheme, which had its origins in the US but was brought to the UK by entrepreneur Richard Tompkins, who recognised the potential of the idea. (He also went on to found Argos.) Shoppers collected one stamp per 6p of shopping and kept track of their collection by sticking them into bespoke books. This job was frequently awarded to children, many of whom, years later, still recall the taste of glue in their mouths from licking the stamps. Completed books could be exchanged for a wide range of consumer goods from toasters to toys and TVs, right up to a Silver Cloud motorboat. Just for context, 217,600 stamps were required for the motorboat, equating to an outlay of £5,440, which at the time was equivalent to the price of a large, detached house.

Despite the huge outlay required for the big rewards, collecting Green Shield Stamps became a huge craze. An article in *The Sunday Express* from November 1963 reported a Tesco store in Leicester being 'besieged by thousands of housewives': 'Twelve women fainted. The staff were completely overwhelmed. Finally store manager John Eastoe cleared the shop and closed all the doors.' (Humby et al 2003)

Not surprisingly, rival retailers quickly saw the opportunity. In fact, a 'stamp war' broke out among grocers in the UK and further afield. Fine Fare adopted the American S&H Pink Stamps, the Co-operative movement launched blue stamps and other chains such as Tesco also began offering Green Shield Stamps. Many local retailers also began offering their own, personalised stamps. It wasn't until the 1970s that the popularity of stamps began to wane and this was as much to do with an economic downturn that caused shoppers to seek out price promotions rather than collect stamps for rewards down the line.

6. Status is a strong motivating force

On 1 May 1981, American Airlines launched AAdvantage, a frequent flyer programme. Members could accrue miles through buying tickets and then redeem them for free tickets, upgrade their ticket class or obtain other services such as free or discounted car rentals or hotel stays. It wasn't the first frequent flyer programme – Texas International Airlines beat American Airlines to it by launching in 1979 – but it quickly became the largest. Today it boasts a membership of 100 million and has expanded to include more than 1,000 partner companies and airlines.

When AAdvantage was launched, the concept received a lot of flak. Commentators couldn't get to grips with how it could be worth an airline's while to give away such valuable rewards. Interestingly, competitors weren't slow to realise the potential. United

Airlines rapidly rolled out its own MileagePlus programme and, today, most airlines are affiliated to one of the many schemes on offer. The reason behind this popularity is that airlines understand that these programmes are about more than simply getting people to book with one particular airline more regularly: they're about status. The programmes are tiered and therefore offer different (and better) rewards, based on milestones crossed by members. The more a member spends or flies, the higher the tier they enter. What really makes this work is that airlines make these tiers visible to everyone, often via a coloured tag that can be attached to luggage. Members can work through, say, a blue or green tag, through to gold and then black. Showing off your status relative to others in the programme plays upon the competitive desire for a higher social standing. Plus, because higher levels come with bigger and better privileges, these tiered schemes make the most valued customers feel the most valuable. They are getting stuff no one else has access to. For many airlines, these programmes have become a crucial part of customer retention strategies, particularly in the fight back against low-cost carriers.

Because higher levels come with bigger and better privileges, these tiered schemes make the most valued customers feel the most valuable.

The idea of status has since been adopted by many loyalty programmes. In the UK, Waitrose launched a scheme whereby members who signed up to myWaitrose were given free coffee in stores. This signified that they were members of this elite group of valued customers. It was a huge promotion, elevating Waitrose to becoming one of the biggest importers of coffee in the country almost overnight. The scheme was scaled down in March 2022 and is now only available to customers who provide their own cups (a maximum of one hot drink on any given day).

7. Make sure you consider all the variables

While loyalty promotions can create powerful bonds with tens of thousands of customers, if they're not properly planned and executed they can also go badly wrong. Before launching a campaign of any scale, organisations need to do some legwork and look at all the variables. Once again there's an abject lesson of what happens when some key pieces of information are overlooked. This one comes courtesy of McDonald's, which celebrated the 1984 Summer Olympic Games in Los Angeles with a promotion giving away freebies for every medal the US team won. Anyone in the United States who bought food or drink from beneath the Golden Arches was rewarded with a scratch card featuring an Olympic event. If the US team won gold in the event revealed on the scratch card, the patron would receive a Big Mac. A silver medal meant free French fries, and a bronze, a soft drink. So far, so patriotic. The promotion, advertised by the motto 'when the US wins, you win', would, it was believed, help American sports and burger fans get behind the games. Except the McDonald's team overlooked one crucial factor. The Soviet Union, then a sports powerhouse, was not participating. The US had boycotted the previous games in Moscow, in protest at Soviet warfare in Afghanistan. So, in a tit-for-tat move, the Soviets gave the American games a miss. For good measure, East Germany and some other socialist nations also followed suit. As a result of the vastly reduced competition, the US medal haul was immense. At the 1976 Olympic Games the country had secured 94 medals (34 gold) but this number rocketed to 174 medals at the Los Angeles Olympics, with 83 gold. In the resulting dash for free fast food, some of their (then) 6,600 American outlets ran out of Big Macs (Hollie 1984).

Before launching a campaign of any scale, organisations need to do some legwork and look at all the variables.

8. The rule of reciprocation

It wasn't until 1984 that we began to better understand the psychology behind loyalty. This was when Robert Cialdini, professor of psychology and marketing at Arizona State University, published his book on persuasion and marketing, *Influence: The Psychology of Persuasion* (1984). One of the six key principles he identified was the rule of reciprocation, which describes the universal tendency of individuals to feel a strong impulse to repay or reciprocate when given a gift.

When customers are rewarded with a gift that they perceive is in their interest rather than the retailer's, it leaves them feeling obliged to return the favour.

What's remarkable about this rule is that the level of reciprocation can be out of all proportion to the value of the gift. One of Cialdini's definitive studies was carried out with McDonald's and found that even the most simple rewards can provoke powerful emotions. (This may have left the fast food giant's bosses wishing they'd taken note ahead of the Olympic promotion.) Every child who visited a branch of McDonald's was given a balloon at the cost of a couple of cents each. Half the children received a balloon on the way in and half were given one on the way out. Those who received the balloon before their meal spent 25 per cent more than those who received their balloon after finishing their burger. There was also an identical uplift in coffee orders. Parents who perceived the balloon as a gift of value on the way to buy their children's meals reciprocated by spending more, treating themselves to a hot drink.

Loyalty programmes provoke an emotional, reciprocal relation-ship between a retailer and its customers. When customers are rewarded with a gift that they perceive is in their interest rather

21

than the retailer's, it leaves them feeling obliged to return the favour. The notion that they're receiving VIP treatment encourages them to believe that the retailer cares about them, which in turn encourages a feeling of belonging. These emotions, combined with enjoying the rewards they earn, make them more likely to return to make further purchases and even recommend the retailer to their friends. It's emotion that powers their decision to continue interacting with the brand over and over again. This rule continues to be used by a number of retail brands today. Multinational brewery and pub chain BrewDog ran a highly successful campaign where they gave away free beer to prospective customers. BAM, a bamboo clothing company, regularly sends free socks to prospective customers along with a 15 per cent discount code. Customers may ignore it the first time but after a while the rule of reciprocity kicks in and they go online to order socks. While they are there, they also order boxers, shirts and sports clothing.

9. Loyalty means much more than simply rewarding customers

Ask any retailer for their view on the biggest milestones in loyalty and it's highly likely they'll name Tesco Clubcard, which appeared on the scene in 1995. It was, said Sir Terry Leahy, a way of 'putting trust in the customer to allow us to strive for some audacious goals'. But it was not simply the customers that Tesco's then marketing director wanted to get closer to. As he later outlined, loyalty meant so much more to the UK grocery giant than rewarding customers. Winning and retaining loyalty was, he said, 'the single best objective any business can have. The search for loyalty is, at its heart, an age-old idea; you reward the behaviour you seek from others.' (Leahy 2012)

Sir Terry's view is that loyalty extends to colleagues, managers, investors and, in fact, any of the retailer's stakeholders – and that it goes so much further than a simple transaction. Based on mutual trust, when it's seen to be acting in everyone's interest it's an attachment that grows and becomes prevalent in every area of a business.

> *Loyalty extends to colleagues, managers, investors and, in fact, any of the retailer's stakeholders.*

Although memorably derided by rival Sainsbury's as no more than an 'electronic Green Shield Stamp', it was obvious to everyone in retail that the Clubcard was a significant development. Indeed, I remember that my initial reaction to the launch and what it might mean to TCC was one of concern. We weren't that worried but could see a big change coming. However, it worked out well. It was complementary to our business because it put loyalty firmly on the map. Also, Terry Leahy talked a lot about values: treating all stakeholders openly, with honesty and respect. Overall, it moved loyalty another step further towards becoming a significant and central part of retail strategy.

Tesco Clubcard was one of loyalty's biggest milestones

One of the best known aspects of the Clubcard was Tesco's partnership with Dunnhumby, a data science company that was able to interrogate the huge amount of data gathered about Tesco customers via the cards. This knowledge changed the way the chain categorised shoppers. Previously, categorisation had been by life stage, lumping together groups such as students, young singles, parents with young children and so on. Now, more authentic classifications were produced, defining people by what they bought. New categories were introduced so that marketing efforts could specifically target people on a budget, vegetarians or devotees of fine food and wine. Armed with this data, Tesco was also able to extend the range of products it offered, moving on to sell insurance for everything from pets to cars as well as mobile phones and banking. At one stage it opened a Tesco Cars operation, offering its then 16 million Tesco Clubcard holders the opportunity to own ex-fleet cars. Trust levels in the brand became so high that it was reported at the time that many customers were happier buying a new car direct from Tesco than they were from their local dealership.

Sir Terry's assertion that loyalty is about so much more than simply rewarding customers is even more pertinent today. Over the past few years, we've seen a huge shift towards what's known as 'people and planet'. Retailers who, until not that long ago, were fixated on price and quality now recognise that they have a responsibility towards their communities and what they care about. Today's stakeholders are the environment, health services and the planet itself. Loyalty has become as much about doing good and giving back as rewarding shoppers with gifts. We've come a long way from the days of wrapping slices of soap in paper printed with coupons!

10. Learn about six key loyalty mechanisms

Customers from almost every region of the world will now be familiar with some sort of loyalty programme. While many promotions still share roots with the ones that went before, they have inevitably become more sophisticated with time. Today, there are essentially six main categories of promotions.

1. Best customer marketing (BCM)

Previously known as a continuity campaign, BCM is now one of the most widely used loyalty mechanisms. Frequent customers earn points or tokens on every purchase, which are saved up to spend on a reward. If they spend more, they receive more. This strategy has the benefit of turning occasional shoppers into frequent visitors and, of course, rewards those high-spending customers who are already loyal. Ideally, the BCM collection mechanism is as simple as possible. Collect one point for every €xx spent. Save up a meaningful number of points and become eligible for a free item. Programmes like this motivate customers to stay with a brand for long enough to accrue the required number of points.

Tiered programmes often work better for high commitment, higher price point purchases such as airlines, hospitality businesses or insurance.

BCM is used extensively in the retail environment, popping up everywhere from superstores to petrol forecourts. They can also be expanded into tiered programmes that offer both short- and long-term value in return for points. Here, customers collect a nominal reward in return for a low number of points but if they continue to collect, they can move up through the tiers, which rewards initial loyalty and encourages further purchases. Tiered programmes often work better for high commitment, higher

BEAUTIFUL CUTLERY FREE

WITH BONUS POINTS

Alessi is a registered trademark used under license by TCC Global N.V., World Trade Center Amsterdam, Zuidplein 84, 1077 XV Amsterdam, The Netherlands

SEE SAVER CARD FOR DETAILS

Design: Ettore Sottsass, 1987

4 piece mocha coffee spoon set
Set di 4 cucchiaini da moka
Set bestehend aus vier Mokkaloeffeln
Set de quatre cuillères à moka
Set de cuatro cucharas para moka

ALESSI

N U O V O   M I L A N O

Free offers are hugely motivating for customers

Branded product rewards can stimulate shopper participation

price point purchases such as airlines, hospitality businesses or insurance. As customers move up through the tiers, they can be given access to exclusive options such as early booking or upgrades.

2. Sport and entertainment campaigns (SEC)

Being a committed fan of a sports team, athletic discipline or film franchise evokes feelings of passion among millions of people around the world and that's especially true for kids. Tapping into that passion by helping people get closer to what they love seems like an obvious strategy for any loyalty campaign. Sports and entertainment campaigns capitalise on the excitement and enthusiasm about our most talked-about events, extending the reach of campaigns. These large-scale campaigns are also the perfect way to reach everyone in the family, as big sporting tournaments such as the World Cup or popular TV shows nearly always bring everyone together. Campaigns like this are usually based around collections that are closely connected with the event they celebrate. This builds upon the strong urge to collect (see lesson 16), where individuals want to become fully immersed in the world of their idols by gathering up as much paraphernalia as they can.

To give you an idea of how significant the scale of an SEC campaign can be, here are some statistics from a 'Feast of Football' campaign we worked on with Sainsbury's to coincide with the 1998 World Cup. Working alongside the English Football Association, World Cup medals were minted with an image of a footballer on one side and the Football Association logo on the reverse. Shoppers could collect one of 23 free medals with every £15 spent on petrol, or with 20 different types of own label products. During the 14-week promotion, incremental sales rose by £21 million, petrol sales increased by 10 per cent and more than 50 million medals and 700,000 albums were distributed. The following year, Sainsbury's won *Retail Week*'s Retail Promotion of the Year award.

This campaign won *Retail Week*'s 'Retail Promotion of the Year' award

3. Community programmes

As previously noted, these 'people and planet', values-based programmes are gaining in popularity among the growing numbers of environmentally and socially aware consumers. The 'values' part of the values-based indicator relates to the internal benefit a customer appreciates rather than the value the programme brings to the business. Here, a retailer will select a charity, campaigning organisation or school that resonates with their customer base. The resulting community programme will then work in a similar way to a BCM campaign, with one key difference: the points earned will be translated into a currency that benefits the community. Community campaigns encourage a sense of pride and accomplishment every time a customer shops. Many of these campaigns pass on significant benefits to the community and today there are examples everywhere you look. Since 2007, global cosmetics chain Lush has raised £53 million with its Charity Pot programme, which has been passed on to grassroots organisations working on animal protection, human rights and environmental issues. TCC itself works with Price Chopper in the US where points can be redeemed against everything from MasterChef cookware to a charitable donation or paying off student loans. (I'll be exploring this in much more detail in Chapter 9.)

The 'values' part of the values-based indicator relates to the internal benefit a customer appreciates rather than the value the programme brings to the business.

4. Consumer games/gamification

While past promotions relied heavily on scratch cards, coupons, stickers and vouchers, times have changed. Since so much of the buying process is digital, it seemed like the natural progression for loyalty to go this way. There are many advantages to gamification. In our more environmentally aware world, digital loyalty cards can often be more eco friendly and, if app-based, unlikely to get lost. Perhaps most of all, though, there are opportunities to be creative. Digital offers an endless number of possibilities to gamify loyalty, where customers can enjoy fulfilling quests to win rewards or 'unlock' benefits by completing actions (and buying goods). It keeps them coming back. We've run more than 300 game campaigns, giving out more than three billion game cards. (I will look at gamification in more detail in lesson 32.)

Digital offers an endless number of possibilities to gamify loyalty, where customers can enjoy fulfilling quests to win rewards or 'unlock' benefits by completing actions (and buying goods).

5. Catalogue programmes

Catalogue campaigns are used less often today but they've changed little from the ones detailed at the beginning of this chapter. They often run for a year or more, inviting shoppers to collect points that can be redeemed from catalogues offering anything up to 70 different rewards or more at varying values, from plasma TVs to a half day at a spa. The downside is that these catalogue programmes can be expensive to run and are often perceived to last too long. When shoppers aren't required to markedly change their behaviour to collect points within a given time, it removes the sense of urgency.

Retailers don't need to stick to one category. It's possible to mix and match. You could, say, gamify a campaign, which offers tiered rewards. Shoppers who 'level up' can reach the next tier. The most common hybrid is a points and tiered system. It's easy to calculate points and there's a clear motivation to move to the next level via further purchases.

There are a few other types of loyalty scheme that are worth noting here. Some are rarely used, while others are specific to the online world. I've included them here in case they come back into fashion or a variation thereof is reintroduced.

Layaway: Shoppers collect receipts, put them in an envelope and once they've reached a pre-set spending requirement, which could be €500, they could take their collected receipts to the checkout to receive a reward.

Spend and get: As the name suggests, shoppers spend a set amount, say €20, and immediately receive a reward. This is similar to piece a week, below.

Piece a week/PAW: A large pallet of say, dinner plates, is placed near the checkout and customers are invited to take one for every €25 spent. So, if they spend €75, they can help themselves to three plates when they buy their groceries. The following week there might be a pallet of cups; the next, a pallet of bowls. This promotion enables shoppers to compile their dinner service week by week, piece by piece. PAW made up the bulk of our business in the early days of TCC but it's relatively rare to see it today because it can be logistically and operationally difficult to run. Despite being piled high with goods, pallets are invariably emptied quickly, which means that someone needs to regularly replenish them. This can become labour intensive for a store.

Subscription loyalty: Subscription loyalty is more common online. Think here of, say, Amazon Prime. By signing up and paying a fee, customers benefit from preferential delivery slots and free shipping. Costco uses a similar model with a membership fee for its discount warehouses. The idea here is to work out which factors may cause customers to go elsewhere and then customise the loyalty programme to help them easily overcome the obstacles.

6. Affinity or coalition programmes

These longer-term programmes are often in place for many years and tend to rely on a major food retailer as the main driver of participation. They will typically have 10 or 20 other non-competing retail partners where shoppers can collect points for varying spend thresholds. Examples of such programmes include Air Miles in Canada or Nectar and Tesco Clubcard in the UK. Other examples are Payback in Germany, Dotz in Brazil and Shares in UAE.

The main characteristic of these programmes is that shoppers can collect points from outlets such as DIY stores, office supplies chains, petrol stations, dry cleaners, coffee chains or travel agencies, etc. Rather like catalogues, they are long-term initiatives that offer myriad rewards, from petrol vouchers and amusement park admissions to spa days, charity donations or shopping vouchers. While they do promote customer loyalty, such programmes are sometimes less effective in changing customer behaviour because in general there's no imminent time limit for collecting or redeeming points.

An important financial aspect of these programmes is the requirement for retailers to pay for the points awarded on issuance rather than on redemption, with obvious consequences for cash flow. Nonetheless, over the past 20 or so years these programmes have continued to occupy an important place in the loyalty marketing space.

Many US supermarket chains offer longer-term gas (petrol) reward programmes that have become ingrained in their promotional calendars. The price of gas in the US is always a hot topic and even though a few cents off a gallon may not seem like much, it's nonetheless seen as an entitlement for large parts of the population. Queuing for discounted gas has become quite a popular hobby.

LOYALTY LEGENDS

The gift of giving: Continente/Carrefour France

Perceived value – or our own personal expectations around a product – can be a powerful driver. Indeed, it's the foundation of most marketing campaigns. Customers believe the reward they're receiving is worth more than its monetary value because it provides such a strong physical, logical or emotional benefit. What, then, if this was put to the test and a physical reward was put up against cold, hard cash? Which offer would win?

This exercise was carried out by Carrefour, a multinational corporation with its headquarters in Massy, France, when it took over rival French chain Promodès in 1999. Prior to the buyout, Promodès operated two facias, a hypermarket chain called Continente and a supermarket called Champion. The acquisition of Continente presented an interesting conundrum for Carrefour. Up until that point, Continente had run a points-based loyalty programme across its 100-store chain and any points its customers collected could be exchanged for cash at the till. Carrefour, on the other hand, didn't offer any sort of loyalty programme at all. Since Continente was being rebranded Carrefour, Carrefour was taking on responsibility for all the points saved up by Continente's customers. It would, overnight, be on the hook to distribute millions of euros to its new shopper base.

The solution tested the notion of perceived value to its limits. Yes, Carrefour customers could still claim the cash value of their Continente rewards. However, they were also offered the option of exchanging their points for physical rewards. A glossy brochure was produced, displaying a wide range of rewards. Each reward was a product from a well-known brand, from Wedgwood to Villeroy & Boch to Tognana. Beside each offer, whether it was 12 champagne flutes or two pieces of a porcelain dinner service, was a prominent reminder of its cash value in bright red letters on a yellow background. The list prices varied from €4 to almost €250. In each, though, the purchase price of the rewards paid by Carrefour was a fraction of the amount.

What was the result? The majority of Continente's previous customers chose the rewards. Carrefour, which had made a provision in its accounts for the cash owed to the loyalty scheme members, saved 38 per cent of the money set aside to repay Continente's points collectors. Case closed: the perceived value of a reward does outweigh the cash equivalent.

2 LESSONS ABOUT CUSTOMER LOYALTY

11. Retaining loyal customers requires creativity

After that brief history lesson, we'll return to the present day. The high street is facing its toughest challenge for a generation. At the time of writing, inflation has hit 11.1 per cent in the UK, which will be catastrophic for many families. The knock-on impact on retailers will be equally tough. Even before the current economic crisis, retail groups around the globe were seeing seismic changes on multiple fronts. After a decade or more of building ever bigger stores, there has been a clear shift in customer preference towards smaller, local ones. According to the website capital.com, customers no longer spend hundreds of dollars, pounds or euros in one visit, preferring the convenience gained from smaller top-up shops (Ruzicka 2021). Smaller shops mean less food waste too, which is essential as we strive for sustainability.

Physical stores are becoming increasingly less relevant as ever greater numbers switch to home delivery. In some regions, the number of virtual shoppers is forecast to double from 2020 to 2025 (Mercatus 2021). Traditional bricks and mortar players have long faced a double challenge with online shopping. Few physical retailers have found a way to make any meaningful profit out of servicing customers online (and for many, it's quite the opposite) while, at the same time, the growth in digital has encouraged countless new internet-only players in the sector, many of whom have become powerful. Digital's share of the grocery market rose by 10 per cent in 2020 and is forecast to double again by 2025 (Gray & Lee 2021). Big tech companies such as Amazon have been scooping up sales across the board from groceries to hardware, a trend that's likely to continue.

Meanwhile, customers have so much more information at their fingertips. These well-informed customers are no longer easily swayed by glossy, marketing-led arguments that one retailer is better than another, particularly when they sell almost identical products. Think, for example, of buying petrol. Most drivers stop their cars at the nearest filling station when they need a top-up. Petrol has become commoditised. While fuel giants still put out the message that their petrol has magic ingredient X in it, the majority barely notice.

The Covid-19 pandemic accelerated these changes even further. Those customers who might previously have loved nothing more than an afternoon pottering around the shops developed the habit of buying and exiting as quickly as possible. Generations that were once cautious about shopping online embraced digital out of necessity and since then have become completely relaxed about filling their virtual baskets with all sorts of goods. In 2020, online retailers increased their total share of retail sales from 16 to 19 per cent. Global ecommerce sales now account for $26.7 trillion of our spending (UNCTAD 2021).

In a rapidly changing world, acquiring and keeping loyal customers has become more important than ever before.

This leaves the world of physical retail in a precarious position. Certainly, no business can take customer loyalty for granted at a time when consumers are becoming more open to adjusting their behaviour. One study found that 30–40 per cent of US consumers have tried a new brand or retailer since the beginning of the pandemic (McKinsey 2021). In a rapidly changing world, acquiring and keeping loyal customers has become more important than ever before. It can be done but it will take some creativity.

12. Loyal customers are worth more to retailers

When we pitched to prospective clients in the early days of the business, I was often asked the same question. Who, they said, is your biggest competitor? My answer was always the same: it's not who, it's what. Our biggest competitor is the special offer. It has been the go-to marketing tool for retailers for as long as anyone can remember and, it seems, can be a difficult habit to shake.

Our view about the effectiveness of this marketing tactic has not changed in 30 years. The focus of retailers who only deploy discounts to keep a customer's attention is too narrow. Customers need to have more reasons to choose one store over another based on something other than pure financial gain.

To properly understand why it's so important to make a meaningful connection with customers, let me take you back in time again to 1991, when TCC was launched in the Netherlands. Back then, the World Wide Web was in its infancy. It would be another three years before the first tentative steps were taken towards online shopping and another year still before Amazon arrived on the scene, albeit in a low-key way as an online bookstore. Bricks and mortar retailers weren't aware of the looming threat but they weren't sitting still. In fact, the focus of retail chains around the world at that time was growth, physical growth. The trend of combining grocery shopping with general merchandise meant that 'big box' stores were proliferating around the world, led by chains from Tesco in the UK to Loblaws in Canada and Carrefour in France to Seiyu in Japan. There was, of course, one essential ingredient required to justify these huge investments: customers – lots of them. It was inevitable that attention would shift to making sure shoppers chose Store A over Store B. Retailers the world over had begun asking themselves similar questions:

▶ What factors influence customers' decision making processes?

▶ How much would it take to help them switch from Store A to Store B?

▶ How do we make sure they don't return to Store A again?

Many, many hours were spent on segmenting customers into tidy little boxes to illustrate their shopping habits so they could be better understood and targeted with more appropriate promotions. These segments would often be presented with memorable names from 'High Spending Whales' and 'Convenience Cod' to 'Scavenger Sharks' and 'Secondary Starfish'. These particular nautical nicknames were coined by Gary E Hawkins, founder of the Green Hills Farms store based in Syracuse, New York and author of *Building the Customer Specific Retail Enterprise* (1979). However, numerous other retailers adopted similar catchy-sounding labels for their segments. Essentially, though, they all boiled down to the same thing. Every store has its own group of high-spending customers – the High Spending Whales in Green Hills Farms' case. Then there are the convenience (Cod) customers who pop in to top up with essential goods. All chains cater for Secondary Starfish, shoppers who aren't loyal to any outlet in particular and who are content to split their shopping between any number of competing stores. And, finally, there are keen-eyed shoppers who will go anywhere where there is a bargain to be had. These are the Scavenger Sharks.

The idea behind such research was to find a way to make a meaningful connection with customers. Ideally, a way would be found to encourage Secondary Starfish and Scavenger Sharks towards more the loyal behaviour of the Convenience Cod or, better still, the High Spending Whales. Why? Because loyal customers are worth more to retailers. The same was true then as it is now:

▶ The top 10 per cent of retail patrons spend up to three times the amount of an average customer (smallbizgenius 2022).

▶ Acquiring a new customer can cost between 5 and 25 times more than retaining an existing customer (Gallo 2014).

▶ Shoppers with an emotional connection to a brand have a 306 per cent higher lifetime value than the average customer (Motista 2019).

To summarise, loyal customers spend more money, visit more frequently and cost retailers less to keep than finding a new customer. Therefore, the priority is to retain high spending, loyal customers. Thirty years ago, when this sort of research was relatively new, I was often surprised that the majority of retailers appeared to ignore the careful segmentation of their shoppers. Instead, they'd gravitate towards the one size fits all style of promotion of, say, 10 cents off a bottle of Coca-Cola or three boxes of washing powder for the price of two. This is classic 'pull' loyalty, prioritising the attraction of customers with a price-led offer. Buying one product means they will get an offer on another, thereby pushing more sales by encouraging them to try something new.

Loyal customers spend more money, visit more frequently and cost retailers less to keep than finding a new customer. Therefore, the priority is to retain high spending, loyal customers.

However, pull loyalty had one glaring fault. Price-led promotions reward everyone who shops at that store, which is all very nice but a waste of money. Customers often had an uneasy sense that these promotions were covered by higher prices on other goods. Most worryingly, these money-off offers reward the very behaviour retailers are trying to get away from. After all, when the promotion ends, rest assured that customers immediately look elsewhere for the next special offer (thanks for nothing, Scavenger Sharks).

Trying to win loyalty via special offers has always been a blunt instrument. It's not always effective in the long or even medium term. It's all very well carefully segmenting customers but the exercise completely ignores the psychology behind shopper behaviour. Science shows us that we largely shop on autopilot. According to shopper psychology studies by the Rheingold Institute, this is known as 'level 1' thinking, which is basically our brain's natural instinct to conserve energy for more rational 'level 2' thinking. If we didn't take these mental shortcuts, known as heuristics, we'd be paralysed by the choice and information overload from aisles full of goods.

In nearly all cases, shoppers have a purely transactional relation-ship with retailers. A shop is there for their convenience and they have no real feelings about the store either way, beyond their habitual behaviour. This is how a rival store can break the status quo with a price-based offer. Since a customer has no real feelings about one store or another, they'll simply go where their goods are cheapest. This isn't disloyalty but apathy. The customer is just as likely to return to their previous store when the discount ends. Discounts and promotions drive short-term sales spikes, briefly breaking habits of existing and rival store customers. Over time, though, the practice has created habits that destroy value and drive promiscuity.

Shoppers expect discounts and 'everyday low prices', so they can never be ignored. However, a big price promotion can cost up to 3 per cent of the value of the sale and some retailers are far better equipped than others for such price-led strategies — perhaps even more so today. You only need to look at the rise and rise of European discounters such as Aldi and Lidl and the impact they've had on the rest of the market. There seems to be less point than ever in focusing the entire marketing effort on special offers when shoppers already know they can get everything cheaper at low-cost chains.

To break conditioned behaviour, the answer is to create new, loyalty-based cue and reward habits that will shape where people choose to shop and how much they spend.

Thirty years on, most large retailers get this. However, they also realise it's impossible to completely turn off the discount tap. Shoppers are addicted to money-off promotions. Thus, canny retailers are careful to give the perception of being 'on it' discount wise but are also broadening their horizons to positively disrupt conditioned behaviour. Old habits do appear to die hard, though. As I saw early on in my pandemic-enforced stay in the UK, there are still attempts at aggressive price promotions. Opening the pages of my Sun newspaper, I saw an advert lining up two trolleys of groceries beside each other, comparing what could be bought at rival grocery chains. I smiled, since it reminded me of trips to US chains three decades earlier, when store entrances invariably featured a trolley stacked with goods, with a sign saying something along the lines of $150 for all this. Beside it would be a trolley credited to a competitor, with a far smaller load for that same $150. I couldn't help but muse that in some ways we hadn't moved forward all that much. To break conditioned behaviour, the answer is to create new, loyalty-based cue and reward habits that will shape where people choose to shop and how much they spend. The goal is to replace the everyday nature of a visit to the store and give it purpose, replacing apathy with advocacy.

13. Make shopping meaningful and rewarding

What every retailer needs to be thinking about in the tough retail environment in which we find ourselves today is: how do we create an emotional connection between us and our customers? How can we make them feel appreciated? The solution is to recognise shoppers as individuals and reward the best, most frequent shoppers with something meaningful (see Figure 1). The offer of a reward makes shoppers feel appreciated, even grateful, for every visit, transforming the retailer–shopper dynamic and significantly reducing the focus on price. Over the years, we have recorded the following positive results for retailers as a result of loyalty campaigns.

Increased frequency: Loyal customers make more purchases, more often. Engaging with a loyalty programme is a conscious choice. When a retailer offers an incentive, a customer commits to shop with them over a number of weeks in exchange for a reward.

Growth in intensity/customer retention: Customers focus more of their shopping activities on stores offering the rewards they covet, making a conscious decision to regularly return to a particular store while shopping less with other stores. Get the mechanic right and the results can be spectacular. We once ran a campaign with BP in Germany offering a free football in return for tokens awarded each time motorists filled their tanks there. Within days of the promotion starting, there were queues of cars outside BP fuel stations, with many drivers driving past near-empty Shell and Esso garages to complete their collection of 10 tokens for their reward. The spectacle even made the TV news. The success of this promotion was quite a feat given, as I said at the outset, that petrol is a commodity today and drivers can and do buy fuel from anywhere.

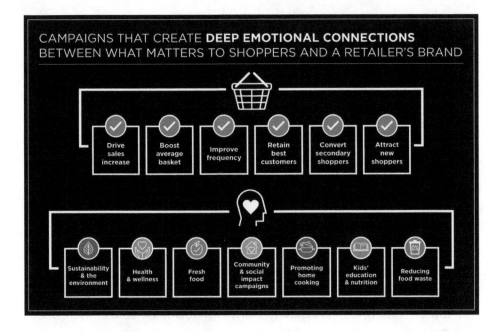

CAMPAIGNS THAT CREATE DEEP EMOTIONAL CONNECTIONS BETWEEN WHAT MATTERS TO SHOPPERS AND A RETAILER'S BRAND

Drive sales increase • Boost average basket • Improve frequency • Retain best customers • Convert secondary shoppers • Attract new shoppers

Sustainability & the environment • Health & wellness • Fresh food • Community & social impact campaigns • Promoting home cooking • Kids' education & nutrition • Reducing food waste

Figure 1 (Source: TCC)

As I said earlier, acquiring a new customer can cost up to five times more than retaining an existing customer and increasing customer retention rates by just 5 per cent has the potential to increase profits by up to 25–95 per cent (Tidey 2018). It's not just easier to sell to long-term customers either; they're also stickier. This translates into being more forgiving when a retailer doesn't quite get it right or fails to meet expectations, which, let's face it, does happen to most organisations now and again. In the introduction, I referred to Store A and how feelings about the UK store were so strong that shoppers would blame themselves for not getting to the store on time if they found an empty shelf.

Another powerful example of this stickiness comes from another UK retailer, Waitrose. In the autumn of 2007 an outbreak of bird flu on two British turkey farms sparked a mass cull in the run-up to Christmas. Waitrose, which had already accepted a number of advanced bookings for organic turkeys, wrote to affected customers to apologise about the unexpected shortage and enclosed a £5 voucher by way of compensation. In the weeks that followed, 80 per cent of those customers returned the vouchers with a 'thanks but no thanks' note. Most touchingly, most requested that the cash be passed onto the turkey farmers to help them at that difficult time.

Once trust is established, in-store loyalty reward programmes have a relaxing effect on price sensitivity, driving top-line sales increases.

Higher spend: Basket sizes increase because, once trust is established, in-store loyalty reward programmes have a relaxing effect on price sensitivity, driving top-line sales increases. Customers become less focused on price and more spontaneous, buying indulgent treats, boosting average spend per basket levels. Visit frequency is also increased. Collecting points encourages customers to spend so they can round up to the nearest euro or dollar to avoid losing out on points.

Reputation building: In-store loyalty rewards programmes create a 'halo effect' around retailers and what they stand for, differentiating them from the competition and encouraging customers to concentrate their spend there. (The retail halo effect is defined by Investopedia as 'a term for a consumer's favouritism toward a line of products due to positive experiences with other products by this maker'.) One way in which many retailers have moved away from the 'price, price, price' message is to stand up for fresh food and get behind the healthy eating message. This was the motivation behind one of our most successful rewards, the Goodness Gang, a collection of fruit and vegetable plush soft toys. Fruit and veg are, of course, at the centre of a healthy diet and these collectable characters reinforce the fresh message (see lesson 44). There are a number of reasons why this is highly effective. It's in a supermarket's commercial interest to maximise their fresh food sales and drive customers towards making meals from scratch rather than buying ready meals. This is where the big margin lies. In addition, the healthy eating message resonates strongly with families today. When a store tries to connect with customers in a personal way, reflecting the issues they're concerned about, the image of a retailer is enhanced. Customers see a well-executed loyalty campaign as a recognition of what concerns them. Therefore, as well as loyalty, these initiatives increase trust and respect.

Word of mouth marketing: A well-run loyalty campaign can create a legion of new brand ambassadors. Or, as one of our collectors so succinctly put it, 'It gives people "bragging rights".' Programmes become a talking point among friends and colleagues, both in person and on social media platforms. Customers who are particularly interested in an offer will recruit friends and family to help them collect points, creating a word of mouth advertising campaign. This is worth its weight in marketing spend, since 92 per cent of people trust word of mouth referrals above any other form of advertising and marketing (Nielsen 2012).

Lasting impact: When a customer knows the layout of a store and it feels familiar, it becomes a habit – and habits are hard to break. Retailers that can tempt a new customer to switch to them thanks to a strong rewards offer should make sure the campaign lasts at least 16 weeks. This is enough to build that long-lasting habit. What's more, the halo effect of the reward is enduring and remains well after a programme has finished. Our in-house research frequently encounters people talking about incentives they've received years, even decades earlier and (most importantly) can name the precise retailer that ran it. Loyalty programmes can genuinely change behaviour in the long term. I recently had a trip down memory lane with the head of Arc, the French glass and tableware group, home to brands such as Luminarc, Arcoroc and Arcopal. We were talking about the petrol station promotions in the 1970s, when tens of millions of tumblers were given away on forecourts by retailers such as Shell. It changed the way many people consumed water in countries such as the UK. Previously, it was more common to use ceramics but with the nation awash with glasses, everyone got into the habit of drinking out of glass tumblers. That habit endured.

Retailers that can tempt a new customer to switch to them thanks to a strong rewards offer should make sure the campaign lasts at least 16 weeks. This is enough to build that long-lasting habit.

14. The halo effect will only work if customers value what's on offer

The obvious retort to what you've read so far is: doesn't everyone do loyalty these days? There are few businesses around the world that don't understand the power of attracting and keeping happy customers. The answer to this is: yes and no. Certainly, there are some countries where pretty much every chain runs some sort of points-based promotion on an ongoing basis. In Italy, for example, where the grocery market is highly fragmented with 30 or so smaller chains rather than a handful of large, dominant ones, it's the norm to run near-continuous loyalty programmes. If the owner of one chain decided to be an outlier and not offer any sort of loyalty reward or, say, start charging a nominal amount for housewares or kitchen knife collections, their customers would inevitably vote with their feet. It's therefore true that shoppers today still get as much of a thrill out of collecting and redeeming points as they did when we first started 30 years ago.

The point to be made here is this: loyalty programmes have to be well conceived and executed to have the positive impacts outlined here. Retailers will only benefit from the halo effect if customers truly value what's being offered. This book is focused on the detail of what it takes to make a lasting impact with physical rewards for loyalty in today's highly competitive and increasingly fragmented market. While many retailers use loyalty schemes to gather data on their customers so that they can better target their offers, let me share what I believe are the four key elements that make for a successful loyalty programme that rewards customers with collectable items. They are:

1. The reward

The reward has to be seen as worthwhile, either free or at an incredible price, with a high perceived value. It has to have mass appeal or be highly collectable. At the same time, it must not feel 'mass produced'. Even though tens of thousands of incentives may be on offer (via the overall promotion), customers still need to feel they're being offered something special. In addition, any reward needs to be in line with a retailer's core values, brand image and shopper base. This part can't be skipped or rushed over. If it is, it can have a negative impact on customer loyalty. This means a retailer has to be certain of the relationship its brand already has with its customers. What is their true perception of the retail brand? By this, I don't mean the one retailers would like them to have. They will need to work on that. No, this means how customers see the brand today. The rewards on offer need to reinforce and live up to these perceptions. Think too about the symbolic impact of the reward. An exercise mat, for example, conveys a message that exercise is worthwhile. Cookware that encourages the preparation of meals from scratch drives home the message of healthy eating and the value of home cooking.

The reward has to be seen as worthwhile, either free or at an incredible price, with a high perceived value.

2. Spend requirement

The spend requirement to redeem a reward should be stretching but achievable. Retailers should set it intelligently, based on current and desired behaviour, to protect the investment. What they shouldn't do is make the reward a mirage where, say, they offer a set of professional knives and all a customer needs to do is spend €10,000 over the next 10 weeks. The price of entry should also be easy to understand. When a customer sees the promotion in-store or hears about it from a friend, they need to believe they can achieve it without pain or inconvenience.

The spend requirement to redeem a reward should be stretching but achievable.

3. Length of promotion

The ideal duration for any rewards promotion is four to six months (in general) and three to four months for sports and entertainment campaigns. In all cases, there should be obvious milestones with rewards along the way to keep customers engaged. The rewards are the incentive; they are what a customer is working towards. They'll be happy to throw an extra item or two into their baskets to reach a certain number of points and realise the reward. However, if they see that it might take a year to earn enough to redeem a €5 gift card, they will never buy into the promotion.

4. In-store execution

The most crucial element that governs the success of a loyalty campaign is the full participation of the stores themselves. Figure 2, below, shows customer awareness of a MasterChef campaign that we ran with a major chain. By far the most important drivers of customer interest all centred around the store and immediately outside. TV and media advertising, which is remarkably expensive, results in a fraction of the response.

MASTERCHEF / THOMAS 'SO CLEAR' PROGRAMME AWARENESS BY CHANNEL

% How did you find out about the programme?   ★ TOP 3 SOURCE

	TOTAL	MALE	FEMALE	18-24	25-34	35-44	45-54
TV Advert	9	6	11	13	9	7	10
Magazine advert	8	4	9	8	8	7	11
Radio advert	6	3	7	3	3	9	8
Outdoor	41	43	40	38	42	43	40
Billboard / outdoor advert	14	13	14	13	14	14	15
Outside the entrance or car park	35 ★	38	34	31	35	36	35
In-store	86	87	86	85	89	85	84
In-store advert	46 ★	47	46	38	46	47	50
In-store display of prizes/rewards	44 ★	48	42	30	47	50	42
In-store promoter	42 ★	47	40	41	43	42	42
Store cashier	26	25	26	20	28	23	30
Store staff	19	25	16	17	20	13	25
Internet	27	28	26	31	28	28	21
Internet: Carrefour website	20	20	20	17	24	22	16
Internet: other website(s)	11	12	10	18	11	9	7
Carrefour WeChat account	28 ★	24	29	32	28	24	29
Carrefour SMS	20	17	21	24	19	19	18
Friends/family (WeChat)	18	19	18	15	20	20	15
Friends/famliy (WOM)	21	16	23	17	22	21	22

Figure 2 (Source: TCC)

By far the most important drivers of customer interest all centred around the store and immediately outside.

Head office can produce all the banners and shelf stickers they like but if the in-store team are not excited about the promotion, they won't put their strength behind it. They may not even put up the promotional material, which means the entire campaign will start badly. Store managers, in particular, need to be brought on board as early as possible (see lesson 27). They have an important role to play, including making sure checkout operators are full of enthusiasm about the rewards so that they remind customers about them and encourage them to start collecting. The way to get consumers to visit a store more often and spend more while they are there is to reward the behaviour you seek. Price promotions can only ever go so far for any retailer. Creating and fostering loyalty will show that retailers care about their customers. In doing so, their customers will care more about them. This is the way to change shopper behaviour.

LOYALTY LEGENDS

The power of free: Intermarché, France

As an international organisation, something that stands out to us is the difference in attitudes to loyalty worldwide. In some regions, such as Italy, campaigns are ubiquitous and it's difficult to find retailers that don't run some sort of rewards campaign. Many do so almost continuously. Elsewhere continuity campaigns can be less frequent. Up until recently, this was certainly the case in France. French shoppers were just as likely to be presented with money-off promotions as any sort of rewards campaign. Up until 2016, retailers such as Intermarché, France's third largest grocer with a market share of 16 per cent, had never tried a loyalty campaign. That was the year we persuaded them to participate in a trial run or, as we put it, assist us in a 'proof of concept' test exercise.

Two promotions were set up. In one, a number of shops acted as a control group, running classic money-off promotions. The other, similar, group of stores ran a rewards programme. The results of the trial were extraordinary. The shops offering rewards saw turnover rise by up to 5 per cent, as well as noticeably increased engagement with shoppers. There were even reports of queues of customers lining up for their rewards.

Buoyed by the success, Intermarché rolled out a loyalty programme across 2,000 of its stores nationwide. In the words of the then Intermarché president Thierry Cotillard, they were now on a rocket ship, shooting for the moon. The reward on offer was seven different types of Pyrex bakeware and the 17-week campaign launched late in 2017. While rewards of this type constituted a fairly traditional sort of campaign for TCC, it was a revelation in this territory. Just as the trial had indicated, shoppers loved the idea of getting something free with their shopping. The results were just as impressive as on the trial. More than 7.5 million pieces of glass bakeware were given away over the period of the promotion to more than two million collectors. Remarkably, the product volumes distributed by Intermarché were three times the amount the manufacturer would normally sell in France during a whole year.

The TCC sales director in the French territory recounts a story of being at an exercise class, listening in to the conversations around her and discovering that all anyone could talk about was the Intermarché campaign. People were comparing notes on how many pieces of Pyrex their companions had collected.

Loyalty has become a stock part of the Intermarché annual marketing effort and the supermarket chain now runs two campaigns a year. Each time they do it they measure an increase in loyalty, engagement and incremental turnover.

The French TCC team that set up the initial campaign won our internal 'campaign of the year' award for their efforts. In a real sign of what an impression it had made on Intermarché, Thierry Cotillard sent a video congratulating the team on their contribution to the campaign, which indeed had taken off like a rocket. He began his speech wearing a space helmet!

3 LESSONS ABOUT CUSTOMER APPRECIATION

15. Don't underestimate the lasting joy of a well-received reward

One of our most successful partnerships ever was with BP, coinciding with the Euro 2004 football championships. I can still vividly remember the pitch for the medal collection to mark the event. Each of the medallions we proposed to produce would feature the name of an individual country, celebrating their participation in the major tournament and could be collected in a BP-branded folder. Every executive in the room appeared to be especially attentive. Indeed, a large number of the marketing team were smiling broadly as we outlined how the promotion would work. I soon discovered why. Each person had a fond memory of a similar football medal collection celebrating the World Cup a few decades earlier. In this case, the promotion was run by rival fuel giant Esso. Esso's coins, featuring members of the national squads, were given away with every four gallons of petrol. The souvenirs had been highly collectable at the time and, as I discovered, had not lost their allure. Many of the people in that room still owned their coveted World Cup coin collection. Some even dug them out of the attic to show me.

The passion for that promotion and the fact that it endured for so long speaks volumes. Yet if you ask any shopper what they would prefer – a cash discount or a reward – they'll invariably say cash. When people tell me this, I always question if that's really the case. Sure, it's nice to get 10 cents off a packet of butter but the feeling of satisfaction about the discount will barely last beyond the time it takes to wheel a trolley out of the chilled food aisle. Yet, as I saw with BP, the joy of a well-received reward can last for years. It's not just football, either. I'm constantly reminded of the power of a diverse range of rewards collections. On a recent visit to Australia, a number of people told me they still owned the dinner sets they collected from a promotion we ran with the Coles supermarket chain more than three decades earlier. How amazing is that? Every time that dinner service appears on their table, it's a reminder of the supermarket that helped them create this lovely setting.

One of my colleagues told me that the amount of appreciation of a physical item was brought home to him by an event we ran in-house at the end of the lockdown. We'd added around 50 new staff to the payroll during the pandemic and none of them had yet met each other or the rest of the team in the flesh. To break the ice, we ran a charity auction in the office, which had the dual advantage that it also raised money for the TCC Foundation (see lesson 50). We auctioned off a number of samples and prototypes from the various campaigns we've run over the years. The excitement this event generated was infectious. There was a frenzy of interest and it was a reminder of the power of real, tactile rewards.

The BP Euro 2004 experience also reinforced something I have long known: we all love collecting. There are few people who didn't collect something as children and many continue to do so in adult life. It's part of the human psyche. I often ask people I meet, 'What do you collect?' People rarely answer, 'Nothing.' They instantly shoot back, 'Coins, stamps, dolls, football cards, typewriters...' – anything and everything.

There are few people who didn't collect something as children and many continue to do so in adult life. It's part of the human psyche.

16. The instinct to collect is a powerful one

What I find most interesting is that the impulse to collect is as strong today as it ever was. If you'd just arrived from, say, Mars, and looked at the practice in purely dispassionate, logical terms, it's likely you'd ask why. Take, as an example, Panini football stickers. In recent years, there has been a succession of stories about the soaring price of these collectables. A sticker of Brazilian football legend Ronaldo from his time at PSV Eindhoven in 1995 would set you back €60,314 if you wanted to buy one today. One of Zinedine Zidane from the 1992 Panini album would cost a mere €39,205 (888sport 2021). Indeed, in 2022, the value of a single football card burst through the $1m barrier for the first time when, according to ESPN, a rare Pele rookie card sold for $1.33 million (Hajducky 2022).

Yet these prices are dwarfed by the value of American baseball cards. These small collectables, with their humble beginnings as cigarette packet inserts used to promote the brand and protect the contents from being crushed, can exchange hands for more than $3 million each (Peng 2022).

On a lesser level, does the average family need another item of cookware, ceramics or a piece of luggage? In most cases, probably not. But do they want it? According to what we've observed over the years, the answer is an emphatic yes, they do. So, to help our Martian visitor and indeed anyone who might be perplexed about why we're all such avid collectors, it might be helpful to look at the psychology behind collecting.

I can still remember the look of incredulity on my colleagues' faces that day. We were having one of those brainstorming meetings, working on a new loyalty campaign for a Spanish supermarket chain called Simago. The brief was clear: we understood the sector and target customer and needed to alight upon a credible reward. I'd done my best tease to build up the sense of anticipation.

'This is the next big phenomenon, guys,' I'd told the team. 'They're already going gangbusters in the US. It's going to be a game changer over here.'

'What is it?' the team asked, all of them hanging on my every word.

'Porcelain dolls,' I announced.

The response was not overwhelmingly positive. In fact, I suspect my colleagues thought I'd lost the plot. Porcelain dolls have been around since the mid-1800s, so were hardly new. At that time, though, they were undergoing another one of their periodic revivals in popularity. Dolls in historical costume were sought after by hobbyists and the type of doll I was proposing was high quality. As with all our rewards, it's crucial that our products are coveted by everyone. Despite the initial doubts of the team, I was proved right. Porcelain dolls were perfect for this market. Within days of launching the rewards programme, Simago saw a noticeable uptick in sales and shoppers seemed very interested in collecting points towards the dolls.

In the interest of full disclosure, I will add that things did get a little out of hand. Stocks of the 12-strong collection were quickly exhausted after demand far outstripped supply. While we'd anticipated a good response, nothing could've prepared us for the scale of it. In a first for TCC, customers began to hang around the store to wait for the next delivery of rewards. When it did arrive, the lorry was besieged by eager collectors. It was mayhem – they were pulling off pallets with their bare hands, climbing over one another to grab the dolls.

So, what does this story tell us? It shows that the instinct to collect is a powerful one. Psychologists have spent a considerable amount of time looking at what motivates the urge to collect (for example, a study by Marquette University investigated consumer collecting behaviour in depth [Spaid 2018]). The conclusion appears to be that there are a number of factors at play here. The first is **value**.

Complete a collection, hang onto it for long enough and big returns are a possibility. Keep it in the attic and one day it will be worth a fortune! We also respond to **rarity**. Specific areas of our brains that are connected to the pleasure centre have been shown to light up when the unusual is presented to us, stimulating the desire to collect. This excitement is further fuelled by the possibility that acquiring this piece will set us apart from our peers, while at the same time encouraging their **recognition** and **admiration** when we display our collection. Collectors who favour antiques clearly feel a sense of history when they assemble items from the past. It may help them to feel more connected with their ancestors, important figures or events from long ago. There could be an accompanying desire to pass on an important **legacy**, to help further generations properly understand the past.

Specific areas of our brains that are connected to the pleasure centre have been shown to light up when the unusual is presented to us, stimulating the desire to collect.

Another strong motivation is to **enhance a social network**. The proliferation of events where people swap collectables from toys and figurines to baseball cards demonstrates this. These often large-scale events are a great way to get together with like-minded people and forge new friendships. This was certainly what we had in mind when we ran a sticker promotion with Ahold Delhaize in Holland, featuring 200 players from the Dutch premier league. Alongside the promotion, we organised a 'swap shop' event in Amsterdam at the Johan Cruyff Arena football stadium. Even we were surprised when more than 10,000 adults and kids turned up to trade their cards.

17. Reconnect customers with their childhood pleasures

One of the strongest motivations around our urge to collect goes back to our early years. As children, we're driven to collect. Not only is it fun and gives us a sense of pride but it's also key to how we learn how to sort and match things. Children build up an understanding of concepts such as 'animals', 'houses' or 'people' by categorising objects. The first time we discover one red Lego brick fits with another is a moment of pure triumph. As we get older and make a conscious choice about whether we prefer to collect and sort toy animals, cars or seashells, we begin to understand the feeling of control. We're also expressing our individuality: I choose to collect this. Feeling like an individual in control of our own destiny is empowering. Once we reach school age, it's normal to back away from that desire for individuality because we want to fit in and be part of a group. Once again, the art of collecting comes into its own. Collect the same items as a peer group and it's a fast track to acceptance in the playground.

While many children show brand awareness from as young as two, the first few years of school are also when children begin to create close emotional connections with particular popular toys. Often, they will favour one brand over and above all others, whether it's Barbie, Hot Wheels or Hello Kitty. Gifts of another in the range of a favourite toy will feature strongly on birthdays and other key occasions. Meanwhile, pocket money will be carefully saved to build the coveted set.

You may feel as if you're a long way away from the child that revelled in their Lego or Hot Wheels collection but the truth is, few of us are. Not in our subconscious minds, anyway. When we begin to collect as adults, what we're also doing is connecting with the child within and becoming more playful. Behaviour and emotions transcend time. The same triggers that made us feel engaged and empowered as children can make us feel the same today. This is the reason why the collectors' market for Barbie, Hot Wheels and Hello Kitty is still so strong today – and often led by adult collectors.

The same triggers that made us feel engaged and empowered as children can make us feel the same today.

One of the most enduringly popular targets for collectors is Barbie. While the iconic doll has come in for criticism since her first appearance in 1959, thanks to her unrealistic body proportions and the lack of diversity in the range, sales of the dolls still top $1.3 billion a year. There's a huge market for vintage collectable versions, with the earliest editions being the most coveted. The so-called 'ponytail number one' first edition Barbie changes hands for upwards of $27,000 today, which is quite a hike from the original retail price of $3 (Caven 2021).

The subconscious desire to reconnect with our childhood is a self-perpetuating process. Parents are instrumental in passing on their own, deeply felt emotions around certain memories. We saw ample evidence of this in one campaign we created that was based on fairy tale characters. They weren't the Disney-style ones that so many of us all grew up with; they were a more up to date, diverse range. However, they still had a similar feel. This was entirely intentional. We knew that a certain generation would be drawn to them, eager to share their nostalgia with their children. Parents were continuing the cycle without even realising it. There are some strong drivers in the desire to collect, relive childhood memories and pass them on to the next generation. This is why we helped Auchan launch a large-scale Harry Potter campaign covering the whole of France in 2021, offering mugs, stuffed toys and trading cards. The generation that grew up with Hogwarts are now parents themselves.

None of this is to forget that children are constantly discovering their own, must-have brands. When TCC first started out, this would've included the then ubiquitous Teenage Mutant Hero

Turtles. A UK promotion we did with the Sun newspaper and the now-defunct Woolworth chain had to be run twice and greatly extended after our initial batch of 10 million Hero Turtles were snapped up almost immediately. More recently, children have been crazy for Angry Birds and Nerf.

Families are a key target group for loyalty promotions, not least because they're the highest spending, most profitable customers in many categories.

Families are a key target group for loyalty promotions, not least because they're the highest spending, most profitable customers in many categories. This is why a great deal of thought is put into creating rewards that will resonate with children. Parents, who make the decision on where to shop, will see collecting these rewards as a simple yet effective way of saying to their sons and daughters, 'I am thinking of you and have bought you something you value.' Plus, of course, most adults instinctively understand that collecting and sorting rewards is crucial for a child's development. It's also preferable to children spending too much time watching television and playing computer games, so it's a win–win.

Children will encourage their parents to shop where the rewards are that they want to collect. They're highly social – more so than any other age group. They also see magic in licensed characters from big film franchises or collectables connected with popular toy brands. Thus, if their friends are collecting, they will want to do so too, so they can talk about the film or the brands to their friends. If someone has the object they want, they'll engineer swaps. They enjoy the fact that everyone in their circle is putting together the same collection (see lesson 34).

As a global organisation, we're often asked whether or not our campaigns vary according to different countries and cultures and the answer is no, not much. It comes back to the foundation of collecting: our childhood pleasure in sorting, matching and trading. Children are the same the world over. They may collect different sets but ultimately, we were all collectors once. The goal is to help shoppers reconnect with the part of their brains that takes them back to when they were five or six. Anything we do that connects us with our childhood has a powerful impact.

18. Make your customers feel seen and feel good

Another of my favourite comments about collecting via our regular customer vox pops came from a woman who was clearly happy about a collection we'd been running in partnership with the American chain Albertsons. When asked how she felt about the retailer that had provided the reward, her answer was simple but to the point: 'I feel seen, appreciated, recognised and rewarded.'

Loyalty programmes are about so much more than getting people into a store and encouraging them to spend more. Their success, or otherwise, is based on how a shopper is made to feel about themselves. The bond is enhanced during each stage of the collecting process, as you can see in Figure 3.

Awareness: When the promotion first launches, some shoppers may not be regulars at the store offering the reward. They have hardly shopped there at all. At this stage, they may register that rewards are available but be reluctant to fully commit.

Consideration: If a store makes enough noise about the offer by flagging it at every opportunity, the overwhelming desire not to miss out on anything free will start to kick in. It will up the ante if family and friends in a shopper's close circle begin to collect and even more so if they post about it on social media.

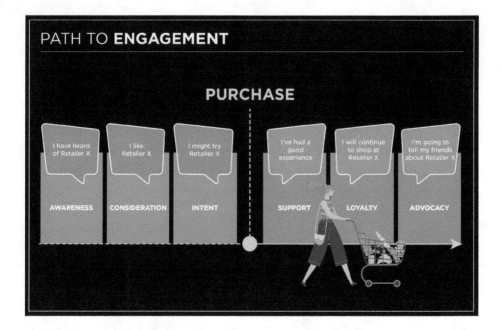

Figure 3 (Source: TCC)

Intent: If the shopper continues to hear about the rewards in a positive way, consideration gives way to intent. 'I can't really go wrong,' a shopper might think. 'Starting won't do any harm.' They resolve to try the retailer and take their first steps to be included in this interesting opportunity.

If the shopper continues to hear about the rewards in a positive way, consideration gives way to intent.

Support: Once a shopper has engaged and taken the first step, such as retaining a sticker, collecting begins to draw them in. With no upfront sign-up involved or payment required, even those who may previously have had reservations about loyalty programmes become more open to the experience. If they're collecting individual pieces rather than points towards a main reward, they'll begin to enjoy adding each subsequent piece to their collection. Even arranging and rearranging it is often hugely motivating. Those who start to fill up lines of stickers will experience the next big driver to enjoying collecting: anticipation.

Anticipation: This nascent stage is where a collector's craving for the object/s in question encourages their imagination to roam. The pleasure centre in their brain will light up as they begin to think about the desired returns an object will bring. It's remarkable how potent this feeling can be. A customer comment that has always stuck with me was from a mum in Hong Kong who literally welled up as she talked about the cooking pot she spent weeks and weeks collecting points for. She intended to use it to cook her son's favourite curry. It was impossible not to be struck by the love and affection with which she talked about her dogged pursuit of this goal. Anticipation isn't something a customer experiences in isolation. Each trip to the store to collect further points towards a reward steadily builds engagement with a retailer. Customers report enjoying more attention from the cashier at the checkout as they discuss the points being earned. This can often prompt interactions with other shoppers at the till. The checkout line becomes more social, friendly and caring – adding to the positive impression in a shopper's mind. Again, this further strengthens the bond with a retailer. Shoppers feel more strongly connected to the community that centres around the store.

Redemption: A key part of this journey is, of course, redemption. We've done a lot of work with the Rheingold Institute in Cologne on the psychology behind a shopper's emotional connection with rewards. After weeks or even months of collecting points, when the customer is finally in a position to claim their reward, they will experience powerful emotions. For many people, the shopping trip that day represents the peak of their excitement about the loyalty programme. It has been called the 'golden moment' – the time when a customer exchanges their loyalty for a tangible reward.

It's important that retailers get this path to engagement right. This is the moment of truth that will define how shoppers feel about the rewards they receive and the store that made it possible. Since one of the key goals is to build a relationship with the retailer, human contact is crucial (see lesson 29). It's a wonderful moment and should be celebrated. It's enjoyable and motivating for the retail team, too. I still vividly remember the time when we accompanied a group from Sainsbury's to pass on the top £1 million reward from their Who Wants to Be a Millionaire? scratch card promotion. The reaction of the winner, a Post Office engineer who had just been made redundant a day or so before, was priceless. If the golden moment fulfils all expectations, the customer is much more likely to come back for more. Customers who reach this redemption stage are eight times as valuable than those who do not. What's more, they're so motivated that they'll increase the rate at which they collect loyalty points by 30 per cent (Ferguson 2017). That's a significant increase in engagement – particularly for any shopper who was initially reluctant to commit.

It's important that retailers get this path to engagement right. This is the moment of truth that will define how shoppers feel about the rewards they receive and the store that made it possible.

Loyalty: Customers don't simply feel a huge amount of pleasure and pride about the objects they collect. They also project these feelings onto the retailers they collect them from and this strengthens the relationship. Another way of looking at this is: rewards are perceived as gifts. We've been brought up to understand that a gift is presented within the context of a relationship. Ergo, this strongly implies that there must, indeed, be a closer relationship with a retailer since it is the gift giver. It creates a deeper bond that might not previously have been there. Shoppers make the decision to continue shopping with the retailer that presented the gift/s. It also doesn't go unnoticed that the retailer is rewarding loyal shopper behaviour rather than prospective shopper behaviour. This is perceived to be the fairer option. After all, individuals hate it when new customers are offered better terms, which does sometimes happen in some sectors such as insurance.

Advocacy: Customers are grateful to a retailer for this tangible thank you. They value that their loyalty has been recognised and show off their reward to their friends, either physically or by posting about it on social media. This is the final part of the journey, from not knowing a retailer at all to trying it and then building a relationship and (literally) reaping the rewards.

19. Boost customer excitement with in-store experiences

Given the emphasis on online shopping these days, it's easy to assume bricks and mortar stores are constantly fighting a rearguard battle. But never, ever underestimate the impact of an in-store experience when it comes to boosting customer loyalty. This applies doubly or trebly when it comes to shouting about a significant collection being on offer. Success here is predicated on the same thought pattern as that followed by major grocery stores during sporting tournaments such as the World Cup. Shops are invariably festooned floor to ceiling with pendants, banners, flags and posters. The message is clear: this store is in the World Cup mood! It resonates with customers, raising the already heightened sense of national fervour around these events, creating a mood of euphoria. Adding a reward tied into the event is the next logical step, enhancing the feeling that everyone shares a mutual interest. It's an open goal, promotions wise.

Never, ever underestimate the impact of an in-store experience when it comes to boosting customer loyalty.

The World Cup only comes around once every four years but that doesn't mean stores need to be devoid of theatre in between. Loyalty programmes are the perfect hook to build up a year-round exciting customer experience. There are some retailers that are absolute masters at this. I would definitely cite McDonald's in this category. Every time you go into a McDonald's, there's a competition or reward on offer and they create events around each promotion. There will be signs everywhere, stickers on the windows, tabletop notices, everything. It's impossible not to get swept up in the excitement. I'm fairly certain they'd get nothing close to this level of engagement if they simply lowered the price of their burgers by a few cents. These regularly changing promotions are effective because they create a purpose and a call to action. Plus, there's lots of entertainment. There are lots of other actions retailers can take to heighten the anticipation behind a loyalty promotion. Many of these ideas will be covered later in the book but to give you a small flavour, there's potential for the following.

Gamification: This is where customers 'unlock' benefits by completing a series of actions. Along the way, they're encouraged to continue to the next stage by the rewards they get for each one, which inspires recurring behaviour. Programme levels can be structured so that customers can see progress and goals that are challenging yet not overly difficult to reach. Constant engagement via gamification prevents anyone becoming bored with the programme. It's also possible to include 'surprise and delight' moments such as random rewards to reinvigorate interest and re-engage any collectors that might be flagging. Even a little win of, say, a can of Coke, will give the customer a positive glow.

'Oh, I won! I never win anything!' is something we often overhear in stores that gamify promotions in this way.

Constant engagement via gamification prevents anyone becoming bored with the programme. It's also possible to include 'surprise and delight' moments such as random rewards to reinvigorate interest and re-engage any collectors that might be flagging.

One of the biggest benefits of gamification is that retailers can gain access to people who may never shop with them at all and attract them into the store. An individual may shop at Store X every single week, without fail. They won't have any connection to petrol station Y because they never fill up there. How does petrol station Y get their attention and tell them about their wonderful in-store loyalty offer? Store X can run a collectable medal promotion, where the first in a series can be collected in-store. Further exclusive medals can be added to the collection via petrol station Y. The link encourages customers to change their behaviour during the period of the promotion. Our statistics show that people who participate in these campaigns travel to stores to pick up their reward within 24 hours of winning it. An impressive 84 per cent of players visit stores more often and four in five spend money in-store while redeeming their prize.

If you were to take it online, a Harry Potter rewards series could be flagged up on social media. Everyone, even shoppers new to a particular retailer, is encouraged to play a game via their smartphone to win. If they get lucky, they need to go to the store and pick up their prize. Most people do go and get that prize, which means Store A has got them through the door, a crucial first step to loyalty. If there are other items available in the collection, a daily social media bulletin will encourage collectors to keep trying. Gamification boosts the core business by bringing in new customers and creating stickiness. (For more on gamification, see lesson 32.)

Educational: Another option popular with parents is any collectables campaign that also offers an educational element. Earlier, we talked about how rewards such as the Goodness Gang have been useful in getting across the healthy eating and fresh food message. Some retailers have expanded their campaign to include Goodness Gang sticker collections. Kids love collecting the stickers and placing them in the albums but it's also a great opportunity to show that fruit and veg are not a chore. The albums feature interesting facts and stories that further reinforce the message.

Nostalgia: As detailed earlier, nostalgia plays a big role in our urge to collect. We've found that some of our best received campaigns have been based on Monopoly or Scrabble games, where customers need to collect a number of pieces to win. McDonald's run a Monopoly promotion every year and have done so since 1987. Back then the rewards had decidedly analogue-style gameplay with the fast food giant distributing tokens that related to properties on a traditional Monopoly board. Over the years, McDonald's has made increasing use of digital in the rewards promotion. Initially customers were rewarded with codes that could be entered online, allowing users one roll on a virtual Monopoly board. Just like in the traditional game, players collected properties and won prizes when all the properties were secured. There have been online innovations with each successive generation of McDonald's Monopoly games, introducing a number of instant win opportunities as well as sweepstakes for grand prizes. What makes this promotion so powerful and enduring is that most people are familiar with this board game, which means they will quickly become engaged. Just like the real game, where it's only possible to win with enough real estate or points, it heightens the sense of competitiveness and excitement. People won't win immediately but if they collect all the cards or properties, they have a chance of winning. It helps too that most customers have a clear understanding of what needs to be achieved to get from start to finish.

For any loyalty programme to be truly effective, retailers need to immerse themselves into the psychology of collecting and understand how customers view rewards. The goal is to create something people covet and inspire them to keep returning to the store over and over again to complete the full set. The journey doesn't begin and end with the reward, though; careful thought needs to be given to every stage of engagement to ensure customers are excited about the promotion and grow even more excited with time.

Careful thought needs to be given to every stage of engagement to ensure customers are excited about the promotion and grow even more excited with time.

LOYALTY LEGENDS

Coveted Kitty: 7-Eleven, Taiwan and Hong Kong

We gained some early insights into the emotional response to a coveted collection via a promotion in Taiwan that centred around Hello Kitty, the much-loved fictional character created by the Japanese company Sanrio. At 200 million units, the number of Hello Kitty fridge magnets made available to collectors in this particular rewards programme seemed ambitious. Yet every single Hello Kitty reward was quickly snapped up by Taiwanese collectors. That's a remarkable figure when one considers that the population of that country is around 23 million. The experience was, however, just a taste of things to come. A similar offer through Hong Kong's 7-Eleven chain became so coveted, it provoked an astonishing response.

The 7-Eleven campaign, which launched in 2010, centred around 22 different Hello Kitty bracelet charms designed in collaboration with Sanrio. For every purchase of 20 HKD, shoppers received one stamp. Once they collected 15 stamps, they were rewarded with one of the charms. The cute charm characters, which had equally endearing names such as Donut Kitty and Apple Kitty, were a massive hit with shoppers. The online app, featuring games and stories about the toys, fuelled the collecting craze and a lively swap market began on social media. There was, however, one episode above all others that sealed just how popular the Hello Kitty charms had become. A thief broke into one of the 7-Eleven stores late one night and the only item they stole was a collector's kit with a full set of charms. The rest of the store's stock was left untouched.

4 LESSONS ABOUT THE COST OF LOYALTY

20. Yes, loyalty does pay

Today, retailers are more beholden to financial targets than ever. Therefore, an obvious question to ask is: does loyalty pay? Short answer: yes, it does. In fact, a well-structured loyalty campaign typically drives a 3–4 per cent lift in total store sales over a 16-week period. Getting into the detail though, can be even more revealing.

A well-structured loyalty campaign typically drives a 3–4 per cent lift in total store sales over a 16-week period.

Thanks to warehouses full of data, retailers have long understood that not all customers are equal. In fact, there's nothing that even comes close to the 'average customer'. As Figure 4 shows, 12 per cent of customers account for 34 per cent of sales. Meanwhile, the low-spending 69 per cent of customers account for 29 per cent of sales. Over the course of a year, the top 12 per cent lay claim to basket sizes that are double, or even triple, the ones bought by the middle 19 per cent of customers who account for 37 per cent of sales. Meanwhile the lowest spenders approach checkouts with baskets that are a fraction of the size of even the middle group of shoppers.

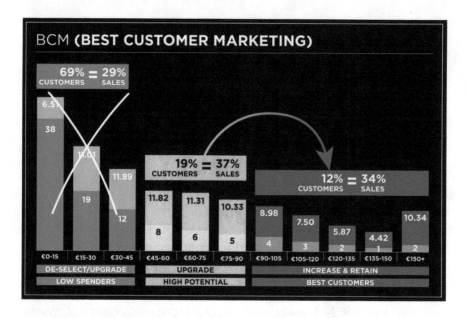

Figure 4 (Source: TCC)

The economics of retailing favours looking after the largest spenders.

More profit per transaction: In all businesses, retail or otherwise, costs are composed of a mix of fixed and variable components. Small transactions carry a higher cost per item than larger ones, where fixed costs can be spread over more items. Therefore, it costs less to service higher-spending customers and the pro rata profit per customer is higher.

Higher average selling price per item: There's a correlation between the level of a customer's total spend and the price of individual items in their basket. According to Brian P Woolf in his book *Customer Specific Marketing* (1996), the average selling price per item chosen by a retailer's top customers is between 20 and 35 per cent higher than its lowest tier of spenders. Higher spenders favour more expensive brands.

Reduced staff costs/output: A basket full of higher-value items translates into fewer goods for checkout staff to handle, leading to shorter checkout times and shorter queues at the tills.

A well thought through and executed loyalty programme enables retailers to reward the behaviour they want to see by focusing their marketing efforts on their best customers or on individuals or families who could become best customers.

Looking at it in purely financial terms, there's a clear opportunity to encourage the best customer group to increase their spend, since they've already demonstrated they're not averse to this. There's also a good chance that the high potential group could be helped to step over into the best customer category, with a small nudge in the right direction in the shape of a worthwhile reason to concentrate their spend with a store for a four to six month period. Meanwhile, less time and effort is expended on low spenders, since it's highly unlikely that this group is going to substantially alter their behaviour. It would be unusual for low-spending individuals to leap into the high-spending category. A well thought through and executed loyalty programme enables retailers to reward the behaviour they want to see by focusing their marketing efforts on their best customers or on individuals or families who could become best customers. It gives customers a worthwhile reason to shop the whole store to achieve the required spend to realise rewards and do so more often.

21. Understand the core financials

To better understand the economics, it helps to start with the basics. For this illustration, we'll use branded housewares, in this case MasterChef. Perhaps understandably, given the obvious correlation, bakeware is one of the most effective loyalty rewards in food retailing and has mass appeal in every region of the world. In this typical promotion, customers are rewarded with one bonus point for every €20 spent at the checkout. Thus, if they spend €40, they'll get two points; €60, three points, and so on. There are a range of rewards on offer for customers to choose from (Figure 5) and the number of rewards they're able to collect depends on their spending over the period of the promotion, which in this case was 16 weeks.

Figure 5 (Source: TCC)

Customers accumulate points week by week and can spend them when they reach certain thresholds, with goods available at a range of 'price' points. In this example, a 2L mixing bowl is free with 20 tokens, which equates to a €400 cumulative spend. To receive a roasting dish, the customer would need to save 30 tokens and therefore spend €600.

An average family shopper will spend €150 per week. If they like the promotion and choose to shop exclusively with the store running it throughout the 16-week period, they'll spend a total of around €2,400, netting 120 tokens in total. This would be enough to collect three or four pieces in the set.

As well as encouraging exclusivity, the dual purpose of the promotion is to motivate shoppers to spend more. The number of tokens required to achieve the Pyrex rewards is therefore set at a threshold that will stretch customer spend by around 10 to 15 per cent if they wish to achieve a larger collection.

It's worth pointing out that Figure 5, which is taken from an actual flyer from a TCC campaign, features two further crucial pieces of information, over and above emphasising the all-important word 'FREE'. One is to note the actual recommended retail price (RRP) of the item, which emphasises its value. Rewards should always have a high perceived value among collectors and this reiterates the desirability of the items. The second point is that there's an option to combine tokens with cash to achieve the reward. Again, the size of sum required reinforces the perception of the high value of the reward on offer.

Rewards should always have a high perceived value among collectors and this reiterates the desirability of the items.

What, then, are the core financials behind this offer from a retailer's point of view? The bakeware represents an 8 per cent reward on shopper spend and the cost of running the campaign equates to 0.5 per cent of total store sales over the 16-week period of the promotion. This includes the cost of the rewards, point of sale material, in-store displays and all the other costs of running the campaign, which I'll explore in more detail in Chapter 5. Assuming the retailer has a 25 per cent gross margin, the break-even point is achieved at 2 per cent of sales (Figure 6). A well-structured campaign will achieve a 3 per cent uplift in sales, or possibly more and a return on investment (ROI) of more than 50 per cent.

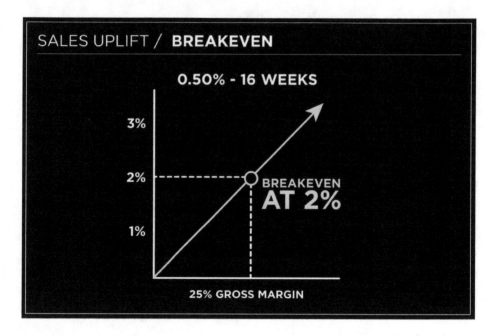

Figure 6 (Source: TCC)

Cash discount versus loyalty

Store A is planning to offer amazing cash discounts across the board for its spring promotion. It anticipates a 6 per cent sales uplift and, to make sure of this, invests a hefty amount into newspaper and digital marketing. It's a success! Store A's sales increase by the expected 6 per cent over the period of the promotion. However, despite the 6 per cent uplift, profits slump. And herein lies the problem: these aggressive price discounts cost retailers what it costs them, ie the full amount of the cash given away. There's also a high likelihood sales will collapse back to previous levels as soon as the discount tap is turned off. As previously noted, short-term promotional giveaways or specials of the month can and do create a spike in interest but this doesn't often translate into a long-term gain. The ideal promotion is, of course, one where both sales and profits increase at the same time plus, ideally, where there's a long-lasting halo effect that keeps customers coming back long after the promotion ends.

So, how does Store B's loyalty promotion compare with the straight cash reward detailed above? As per Figure 7 below, if Store A's price discount promotion is giving shoppers back the equivalent of €1 for every €100 spent (1 per cent – although strictly speaking, the cost of a cash reward is 0.75 per cent if the retailer makes 25 per cent margin on the food the shopper uses the voucher on), it would typically need a 4 per cent sales lift just to break even. If you take the normal retail value of a loyalty reward, it typically amounts to 5–8 per cent per €100 spent, which goes to the customer as their reward – rewarding them with something that is up to eight times the value of the straight cash reward. With the same level of investment, the actual cost to Store B to achieve this is half of the straight cash reward of Store A. Similarly, the break-even point of just 2 per cent for Store B's rewards programme is exactly half of that of Store A's cash reward plus shoppers receive a higher-value promotions incentive.

PRODUCT REWARDS **VS CASH REWARDS**

	LOYALTY PROGRAMME STORE B	CASH REWARD STORE A
REWARD PER €100 SPEND	5-8%	1%
COST	0.5%	1%
SALES UPLIFT NEEDED TO BREAKEVEN	2%	4%

Figure 7 (Source: TCC)

According to our own figures, discounts such as those offered by Store A can encourage customers to spend 10–15 per cent more. They create a sense of urgency: buy it now before the promotion is over. (Although, arguably, Store A is losing further profits via lower margins during the discount period, which may impact sales later on if customers have stockpiled goods.) How, though, does loyalty encourage customers to spend more over the period of the promotion? To illustrate this, we'll look in more detail at Store B's promotion. (The example is based on an actual programme at a major European retailer.) As Figure 8 shows, this retailer's promotion centred around an offer of a five-piece set of saucepans worth a total of €100, which a customer could receive for free provided they spent a qualifying amount in-store.

Figure 8 (Source: TCC)

Before the promotion went live, just 678 customers were achieving the required spend per shopping trip to qualify for the offer. However, after the promotion was launched, 3,577 shoppers went on to redeem the free sets. (We call this 'customer participation', which is the percentage of sales represented by the people taking part in the programme.) This equates to a 428 per cent increase in the number of customers spending more than €175 per week. Many of these 3,577 now high-spending customers previously spent far lower amounts in-store. Therefore, they were not just 'locked in' to the retailer over the 12-week period of the promotion, they were also encouraged to regularly spend more, resulting in a 5.6 per cent sales increase.

THE **OUTCOME**

OFFER	SPEND PER WEEK REQUIRED TO OBTAIN OFFER	NO. OF CUSTOMERS SPENDING AT THIS LEVEL (STORE DATA)	ACTUAL REDEMPIONS	% CHANGE
FREE	**€175+**	**678**	**3577**	**+428%**
SAVE €125	€140	1084	822	-24%
SAVE €95	€105	2169	329	-85%
SAVE €60	€70	3253	113	-96%

Figure 9 (Source: TCC)

While the Store A/Store B comparison is purely financial, there are other metrics by which to evaluate the effectiveness of any loyalty campaign and there are often wide regional variations. In the US, for example, there's a tendency to measure them using short-term indicators such as growth in sales volume and average sales receipts. This is in line with the nation's usual assessment of management performance by the means of economic and financial ratios such as ROI and stock turnover. In other regions, retailers may place more importance on less tangible results such as improved image and consumer trust. We see evidence of this in Italy in particular.

Campaigns can also be run to answer specific business strategies such as increasing sales in a particular segment. This was a strategy deployed by Asda Walmart when it set a goal to grow own label sales to a clearly defined level that represented a significant proportion of overall revenues. The loyalty promotion we designed with them had a gamified theme which, as well as offering rewards, also provided customers with the chance to win a year's worth of free groceries if they correctly answered a questionnaire about the quality of Asda Walmart's own label products. The beauty of this mechanic was that customers needed to find out more about own label products to be in with a chance of winning the big prize. The promotion was judged a success since it played a key part in taking Asda Walmart's own label penetration well above the target level.

Campaigns can also be run to answer specific business strategies such as increasing sales in a particular segment.

Other strategies campaigns can help with include:

▶ driving strong top-line sales increases +3 per cent

▶ improving visit frequency

▶ retaining best customers

▶ converting secondary shoppers

▶ attracting new or lapsed shoppers

▶ strengthening brand advocacy

▶ combating new competition.

Plus, of course there are softer KPIs, which include supporting initiatives such as:

▶ sustainability and the environment

▶ health and wellness

▶ recycling of plastics

▶ promoting home cooking

▶ driving fresh and centre store goods

▶ reducing food waste

▶ children's education and nutrition

▶ community and social impact

▶ making shopping fun.

22. Understand the cost to retailers

Understanding the monetary value and ROI of a loyalty programme can go a long way in shaping a business strategy and budget. It's impossible to do this, though, without understanding the costs to the retailer. Here are the main elements to consider.

The rewards: Early on, when loyalty was still a relatively unknown and largely misunderstood practice, one of the most common responses we received to TCC's initial pitches was: why don't we do it ourselves? The thinking went: we are, say, a large supermarket chain, so already have a department skilled in buying homeware/ soft toys/electrical goods. And that's true. Except they've never dealt in the scale of goods required for a credible loyalty scheme or the logistics involved. Retailers will be dealing with huge numbers of rewards in many a loyalty programme. Taking the above example of MasterChef cookware, most shoppers will collect three or four pieces, or even a full set. Even for a relatively small chain operating in a single region this translates into the need to buy four or five million pieces of cookware at a time. The world's biggest chains aren't used to buying at this sort of scale. However, this does mean that there's a significant potential for discounts via bulk ordering.

The calculations around how many pieces are required can be complex. Retailers will be asking a shopper to spend anything from €10 to €150 to receive a gift. They will also be encouraged to stretch their shopping budget to spend more so they can collect more tokens towards the collection. How then, with so many variables, does a retailer work out how many rewards to buy? Is it 25 million, 50 million or 75 million? Ultimately it will still involve prediction and forecast as opposed to hard and fast science but it still means buying a large number of rewards. This is why it's useful to work with an experienced business.

The most cost-effective route to promoting a loyalty programme is via in-store campaigns, posters and flyers and participation of the team on the shop floor.

Marketing and advertising: Many retailers choose to incorporate their loyalty programmes in their TV marketing campaigns and this certainly wouldn't be discouraged because it does boost awareness. However, it's an expensive boost. Plus, there's the added consideration that a large amount of the TV spend can be wasted because viewers won't live close enough to the store in question to take advantage of the rewards on offer. The most cost-effective route to promoting a loyalty programme is via in-store campaigns, posters and flyers and participation of the team on the shop floor, which all cost a fraction of what's required for TV campaigns. In addition, one of the most powerful promotions there is comes free of charge: word of mouth. If the offer is right, the local community will talk about it among themselves and encourage others to participate. This can be particularly effective in regions such as Asia, where extended families tend to live closely together. When shoppers discuss a loyalty offer between themselves, it can be 10 times more powerful than paid-for slots.

There is also a (far too little used) opportunity to maximise marketing spend. After many decades in this business, it won't be a surprise to anyone that we are keen observers of developments in the retail world. Whenever we hear that Retailer A is about to become a proud sponsor of an Olympic team, or a series of Bake Off or MasterChef, we're on full alert. This is a huge opportunity, marketing wise, which is why retailers pay the big bucks for these tie-ins. Yet, all too often, the collaboration appears to end somewhere around a nod in the programme notes or a TV credit: Retailer A is the proud sponsor of... To us, this is such a wasted opportunity. Why not extend the promotion in-store, with relevant rewards celebrating the sponsorship from sports team medals collections to cookware ranges? This is what will bring sponsorship alive. Every retailer I know is sponsoring something, yet too few appear to make this obvious connection and fully leverage the link.

LOYALTY LEGENDS

Mixing with a new market: Grundig – Real Germany/worldwide

One of the most remarkable aspects of the continuity business is the sheer scale of it. At TCC, we can safely boast that we're one of the biggest buyers of certain products in the world. As you will have observed in some of the examples in this book, most promotions give away millions of rewards at a time. As well as making a powerful offer for retailers, the process, of course, represents significant branding potential for the companies that manufacture and sell these rewards. It was not an opportunity that escaped the attention of German consumer electronics giant Grundig. The business, which began operating in 1945, made its name through manufacturing TV and radio before moving into telephones in the 1990s. Fast-forward to 2010 and Grundig was on the verge of entering an entirely new market: home appliances. The challenge the organisation faced was this: how do you convince households to buy a Grundig hand blender when they're used to seeing the brand name on TVs and radios?

Grundig decided the answer lay in a large-scale rewards promotion and went into partnership with the hypermarket chain Real Germany for a campaign that launched in the summer of 2010. The promotion, which centred around a points collection for seven Grundig kitchen gadgets, saw more than 2.8 million pieces redeemed. As a result, awareness of the new Grundig home appliances range soared in Germany.

Buoyed by the success of the initiative, Grundig followed up with a further 29 continuity campaigns across the globe. During this time, more than 11 million Grundig home appliances found their way into people's homes via points-based collections. There was, still, however clearly an appetite for more. Once consumers became accustomed to the idea of using Grundig products in their kitchens thanks to the rewards programme, they fully embraced the brand. In Europe alone, Grundig's share of hand mixers rose from 0 per cent to more than 10 per cent in the period following the promotion.

5 LESSONS ABOUT DESIGNING A LOYALTY CAMPAIGN

23. Start by defining the business objectives

In by far the majority of cases, TCC delivers the complete package to our retail clients. By this I mean that we organise the campaign, source the rewards and ensure the programme is properly executed. This includes suggesting the type of reward that best fits with the brand's objectives. But on one memorable occasion this was nearly not the case. For some years we'd been working with a particular newspaper whose high-profile editor was well known for being somewhat outspoken. The day after Princess Diana died, this editor called us. 'We've got to do a Diana coin collection,' he insisted. 'Or Diana dolls. How quickly can we do this?' We had to talk him round to the fact that we'd need to leave an appropriately respectful gap before we did anything of that nature. If we were seen to be cashing in on the death of the princess, it could have easily backfired. (I should add that this note of dignity was not shared by numerous other organisations, who rapidly did something similar.)

The point of recounting this story is to emphasise the fact that the choice of reward and the execution of the campaign are crucial to the success of the promotion. Since the goal is to deliver truly concrete and measurable results, any loyalty programme needs to be a grounded part of the business strategy. Thus, retailers need to be clear about their business objectives and how the campaign will meet those objectives, while also complementing and enhancing the brand.

Retailers need to be clear about their business objectives and how the campaign will meet those objectives, while also complementing and enhancing the brand.

As previously outlined, campaigns are designed to reward the highest-spending customers, attract individuals or families who could easily become best customers and motivate family members and friends who may never have shopped with a store before. They encourage a higher spend and set up the habit of shopping at a particular store. Rewards programmes can also be built around specific strategic goals. For example, some retailers use this type of strategy to signal that they understand and support the issues that are important to the customer base at that moment. In recent times, this means a campaign may have been used to:

► set out a retailer's credentials around areas such as sustainability, health and wellness or home cooking

► raise a retailer's standing in each local area with community-focused and social impact campaigns

► support and drive home single issues such as the drive to increase recycling or reduce food waste.

Alternatively, retailers may use campaigns to meet and reinforce strategic goals specific to their own business and marketing strategies. They may wish to:

► increase performance in specific areas such as fresh food

► improve perceptions of the overall shopping experience

► create a more family-friendly persona.

Once business objectives have been clearly defined, the next step is to move on to design and implementation. Here, there needs to be a clear understanding of what, from a customer's point of view, they want out of a rewards campaign. Fortunately, this is fairly simple and straightforward. In fact, it can be boiled down to three simple questions:

▶ What do I get?

▶ What do I have to do?

▶ Is it worth it?

24. Understand the four pillars of a successful campaign

The answers to the above questions lead to the four pillars of a successful loyalty campaign: offer/reward, spend requirement, duration and frequency, and execution. Thus, a retailer must offer a reward that resonates with customers, clearly set out what the customer needs to do to realise the reward and then ensure the execution of the campaign is seamless. Let's look at the four pillars in more detail.

A retailer must offer a reward that resonates with customers, clearly set out what the customer needs to do to realise the reward and then ensure the execution of the campaign is seamless.

Free or Gratuit - the message is consistently strong in any language

Pillar 1: Offer/reward

What would make your customers happy? It's a simple question but it gets straight to the heart of choosing the right reward. The characteristics to consider are as follows:

The offer: Three of the most emotive words in the English language are win, save and free. Since we're not talking about competition or money-off offers, in the context of loyalty the most pertinent word is free. Why is free so powerful? Because free is a thank you; free is a gift. It makes customers feel recognised. When they receive something

The power of 'Free' when linked to a high-profile brand

for nothing, not only will they feel the need to reciprocate but they'll also be reminded of the excitement at receiving their reward every time they use it. That piece of cookware they use each day in the kitchen or the garden chair they sit on during warm evenings will act like a daily call to action to revisit that same retailer. Even if a reward costs as little as a few cents, it's not the same as free. It will have a completely different resonance. Consider this from your own viewpoint. Which offer gives you the strongest emotional reaction? A store offering a price discount from €2 to €1, or one from €1 to zero? It'll be the latter every time because options with no downside or cost trigger a more positive response. Nothing beats the psychological pulling power of getting something for nothing.

Collectable: As discussed in lesson 16, the urge to collect is hard to resist, particularly so with kitchen items. A powerful motivator for all collectors is the urge to acquire coveted items at a modest price to complete a collection. As well as enjoying the thrill of collecting, they take pride in being so astute. Since the rewards in the programme will either be free or at a nominal cost, this will make the collection even more enticing.

Daily use: The frequency with which the reward is likely to be used is crucial. Imagine customers collecting their dinnerware from Shop B. Now, every time they bring out that dinner service they will be reminded of Shop B and the 'thank you' reward they received. Shop B won't just benefit from the halo effect of providing this free dinner service but thanks to the power of connection, customers will begin to associate Shop B with feeling happy and relaxed. These are the same feelings they have about eating with their loved ones and doing what they enjoy. When that emotion relates to a retailer, it's extremely binding.

High perceived value: Perception plays a key role in the success of loyalty campaigns. Perception is, of course, our understanding or impression of something. In the case of loyalty, if the benefit the customer expects to receive from collecting points is higher than

A selection of TCC's brand partners

their perception of the cost of the reward, that product will have a positive perceived value. When a customer believes they're receiving a valuable product for a small shift in their behaviour, they will get more enjoyment from it. This is another reason why it's good for retailers to offer branded goods (but only if the brand is available at fair/reasonable cost) since brands already have a solid reputation, which by implication will improve the perception of value and therefore appreciation of the link.

TCC has also developed many hugely successful own label brands over the years, which have a global reputation and unit sales in the many millions. These own label brands are particularly effective with regard to optimising ROI and are often more commercially flexible versus some national brands.

A cautionary note on the use of some brands is that high licence fees can negate the offer and ROI. TCC works with brands to deliver an aggressive free offer and impressive results.

For a classic example of how powerful perceived value can be, let me share a promotion we did with a supermarket chain in Texas. For every $1 spent, shoppers received one point. A collection of 600 points could be exchanged for $3 off fuel, grocery items valued at $6 or a chef's knife valued at $29. While the actual cost to the supermarket was the same in each case and shoppers needed an equal number of points for each one, an overwhelming 75 per cent of shoppers went for the knives, while 18 per cent opted for the groceries and 7 per cent for the fuel.

Refreshing: If something works well once, it may be tempting to repeat the strategy. However, offering the same rewards over and over again is not going to appeal to all your customers. Besides, there are limits to how many pieces of cookware anyone wants, even if they're free. Varying rewards will keep customers engaged.

Varying rewards will keep customers engaged.

Branding: There's a reason why big brands spend millions on marketing to build their reputation. A well-known brand's strong core message removes the need for a customer to carefully check that it does what they want it to do. Whenever they see brand X, they know what to expect, whether it's good quality, reliable, consistent or great value. It's the shorthand to show that this offer is the best choice. This is relevant in loyalty, too. Customers will instantly covet rewards from brands they recognise. If a retailer is offering something from Alessi, Warner Bros, MasterChef or Royal Doulton, shoppers will be interested from the start because they will know that it's worth collecting points to gain access to these trusted brands.

Widespread appeal: Retailers that are planning to run a campaign across territories should also consider if the rewards on offer have appeal to customers across all of them.

Mass appeal: Some rewards are more covetable than others. Housewares, for example, are always in demand, whereas cosmetics are based more on personal choice. If the offer centres around a small number of rewards, they must have mass appeal or the promotion will be a flop.

If the offer centres around a small number of rewards, they must have mass appeal or the promotion will be a flop.

Number of rewards included in the programme: Thought also needs to be given to the number and assortment of rewards featured in a single campaign. If the programme seems too complicated or there are too many rewards to collect, people won't want to take part. (Not to mention the logistical nightmare for the retailer, which has to import, stock and manage the vast range of merchandise.) If the range of rewards on offer is too limited, shoppers will collect them too quickly and the programme will be over before it has started. This means there's no point to it because it won't have done its job and created any loyalty. As a rule of thumb, if it's anticipated that shoppers are likely to collect two or three pieces over the period of a promotion, then there should be two to three times this number of different but related styles available so that there's some choice when they come to pick up their reward.

If the programme seems too complicated or there are too many rewards to collect, people won't want to take part.

For inspiration on offers/rewards, here's a list of some of the rewards ranges we've seen or tried ourselves over the years, most of which meet the above criteria:

- artificial flowers
- back to school kits, satchels/backpacks
- baseball cap collections
- barbecues and accessories
- bed sheets and duvets
- bikes and scooters
- candles (scented)
- car storage kits and grocery boxes
- CDs and tapes
- charitable donations
- cosmetics (creams and soaps)
- cushions collection
- deckchairs, beach towels and straw hats

- ▶ dog and cat accessories (bowls/leads/toys)

- ▶ dog outfits (by Karl Lagerfeld!)

- ▶ electric drill collection (Bosch)

- ▶ encyclopaedias and kids' books (Sesame Street)

- ▶ food and drink (gourmet items and wine)

- ▶ footballs, tennis balls and golf balls

- ▶ furniture (indoor or outdoor)

- ▶ garden accessories (Gardena)

- ▶ hairdryers and bathroom accessories (mirrors)

- ▶ handbags, purses, wallets and sunglasses

- ▶ headphones, speakers and chargers (Philips)

- ▶ home and car insurance

- ▶ ironing boards and kitchen cleaners

- ▶ jewellery

- ▶ lightbulbs (low energy Philips)

- ▶ lithograph collections

- ▶ mattresses and pillows

- ▶ perfume collections

- ▶ petrol vouchers/discounts

- ▶ picnic chair collection

- ▶ picture frames

- ▶ porcelain dolls

- ▶ rug and carpet collection

- ▶ scarves collection

- ▶ socks collection (including one made from used tea bags)

- ▶ song downloads

- ▶ spa days/amusement park vouchers

▶ tablecloths

▶ teddy bears (traditional)

▶ tents and sleeping bags

▶ tool collection (screwdrivers and wrenches)

▶ T-shirts (featuring endangered species)

▶ umbrellas

▶ video downloads and DVDs

▶ watches (Snoopy and Disney branded)

▶ yoga mats and dumbbells.

There's an element of subjectiveness about this and, occasionally, despite each promotion fully meeting its brief and every instinct saying this is going to be a slam-dunk success, it won't be. One of our most memorable examples was when we had the idea of bringing the concept of porcelain dolls up to date by dressing them in Dolce & Gabbana and Gucci outfits. Dolls had always been hugely successful in the past and this felt like a perfect brand match for the retailer involved. It wasn't. For some reason, the idea, while popular, didn't gain the traction we'd expected and the idea was dropped.

Alternatively, a campaign might be a massive hit but not in the way you'd expected. I'm thinking here of a promotion we worked on with Italy's largest grocer, Conad. The reward had a wine drinking theme with a giveaway of wine glasses. The 'big ticket' item, for which the most points were needed, was a fine-looking carafe for red wine. Our initial calculation was that no more than 50,000 carafes would be distributed throughout the period of the promotion. Almost overnight, it went crazy. In the south of Italy in particular, we could barely get the carafes to Conad's shops quickly enough. For a while, we were completely perplexed. When we looked into it, we discovered why. A fashion had developed for using the carafes as stylish and unusual vases for summer flowers. The trend had spread like wildfire. The point here is that not every idea will be a success, or at least, not in the way you might have predicted. However, if you follow these four pillars, it's highly likely that it will make a significant impact.

Pillar 2: Spend requirement

The reward is not, of course, completely free. The other side of the bargain is that customers need to spend a certain amount to collect tokens or points towards their free gift. Therefore, to fulfil the second pillar of the loyalty campaign, that spend amount needs to be fixed. This means finding answers to two questions:

► How many points do customers need to collect to realise their reward/s?

► How many pieces will be on offer and at what level will the required spend be set?

In all cases, the spend should be stretching for the highest-spending customers but also achievable. To return to our average family that spends €150 a week, it's not too ambitious to expect them to spend €2,000 over the 16-week period of the promotion to achieve the required level, since it would actually mean a drop in their weekly spend to €125. It simply means they'd have to concentrate the majority of their spend with just one retailer. However, if they're asked to spend €4,000 over the same period to redeem the reward, that would in some cases be too challenging. This would involve increasing their weekly spend to €250.

If it seems like too much of a stretch, customers simply won't bother. We saw evidence of this among petrol retailers some years ago. Many began offering free towels and homewares in return for a certain amount of spend on fuel. However, the spend was pegged far too high. Motorists quickly worked out they'd need to drive extraordinary distances to achieve the rewards and, unsur-prisingly, rejected the offer.

If collectors aren't stretched enough, there's no incentive to change their habits which is, after all, the objective of the programme.

The other end of the scale is when the spend is too easy. If collectors aren't stretched enough, there's no incentive to change their habits which is, after all, the objective of the programme. Even worse is when retailers completely under-price the spend, which can turn into a costly exercise. UK supermarket Tesco had a taste of this with a loyalty promotion on bananas. In 1997, the supermarket group offered 25 Clubcard points, then worth £1.25, in return for a customer buying a pound of bananas, costing £1.17. A physicist called Phil Calcott saw the obvious flaw in the offer and bought 1,000 lb of the fruit, giving it all away to passers-by outside the shop. He made a profit of £25.12 before shop staff stepped in and stopped taking any more bulk orders (see Smith 1997).

Pillar 3: Duration and frequency

As detailed in Chapter 1, many early loyalty promotions adopted an open-ended, catalogue-style mechanism where gifts could be collected once a customer had amassed enough points. There would be a choice of hundreds, even a thousand, different rewards. While it's always great to be offered a choice, this isn't always the most effective form of loyalty, which is why it's less common to see such schemes today. Not only is it daunting for any customer to have to collect thousands of points to get the object they desire but there's also the case that with no clearly defined end date, there's no urgency to the offer. The collections process can easily drift. Customers begin to think, 'I'll go back in a couple of weeks but for now it's more convenient to shop at another store.' This means the habit-forming bond of loyalty that the retailer is trying to create is easily broken.

We live in a complex world, so simpler campaigns can be more effective. Make sure it's obvious what a customer has to do and offer a well-defined timeframe in which they have to do it to achieve the rewards they covet. The duration of each rewards programme should reflect the calculations that have already been made on spend threshold. If, therefore, an average shopper spends €150 a week, how many weeks will they need to shop to collect three or four rewards? Again, the timescale should be a stretch but it can't be too demanding. Generally, this will be between 12 and 16 weeks but 20 weeks can also be a reasonable period.

Make sure it's obvious what a customer has to do and offer a well-defined timeframe in which they have to do it to achieve the rewards they covet.

When deciding upon the duration of programmes, consideration should also be given to frequency or how many different campaigns might run each year, so there's a suitable gap in between. There are some regions, such as Italy, where it's the norm to run rewards programmes all year round. Elsewhere, it's more common for retailers to run major rewards programmes just once or twice a year. The benefit of these intermittent programmes is the anticipation that can be generated leading up to the next reward giveaway. It's particularly useful to link promotions with the run up to big annual events such as Christmas, Chinese New Year or Thanksgiving, times when customers spend more than usual on food, drink and gifts. Anticipation is a powerful emotion. A well-executed campaign can be launched three months ahead of the crucial event, building customer traffic and helping customers get locked into the habit of shopping at a particular store. Thus, when it comes to choosing where to shop for these celebrations, they will inevitably go to the store where they are now accustomed to shopping.

The benefit of these intermittent programmes is the anticipation that can be generated leading up to the next reward giveaway.

Pillar 4: Execution

This final pillar is key. Everything needs to be in place before the campaign begins because trying to put things right when the key issues have not been properly agreed and addressed upfront will rarely lead to a successful outcome. There are so many stories of great-sounding promotions that went horribly wrong because one small yet crucial detail was overlooked.

Everything needs to be in place before the campaign begins because trying to put things right when the key issues have not been properly agreed and addressed upfront will rarely lead to a successful outcome.

Managing rewards stock: It would be easy to imagine that with the rise of 'just in time' manufacturing, it would be easier to trial a campaign, see how it goes and order more rewards as necessary. Unfortunately, this is not the case. Shipping lead times from countries such as China are getting longer. Therefore, before the campaign begins, there needs to be an accurate idea of the number of rewards required and a proper supply channel agreed. There may also be an argument for pinpointing a number of sources for stock. We worked with a retailer in Sicily that was keen to offer an exclusive range of pottery made in Stoke-on-Trent in the UK. The range of rewards quickly became a huge hit with customers but disaster struck when the ceramics factory was razed to the ground following a fire and the kiln used for making the pottery was no longer operational. The rewards programme was immediately halted on the grounds that no more stock was forthcoming, nor was it likely to be for some months. There were near riots in the store when the news broke. Shoppers were so disgusted that they weren't able to collect their rewards that they abandoned trolleys full of food at the cash desks. One of my colleagues was summoned to Sicily to explain himself to 20 regional managers at head office. They'd set out the room with a circle of chairs, with one in the middle for him. It was, he recalls, quite an experience. There is, of course, no way to completely guard against unexpected occurrences like this. It is, however, prudent to spread the risk and ensure that rewards can be sourced elsewhere in an emergency.

Clearly defined collection process: Every step of the collection process needs to be properly defined. Customers need to understand how to reach each goal.

Checks and controls: Nothing can be left to chance. What would happen if, say, there's an error at the printing stage? Instead of ensuring there's just one chance to win a grand prize, what if numerous cards were issued offering the same reward? This happened to a major supermarket in France, which ran a campaign to win a car and, in the first 10 days of the campaign, 22 people won. But they only had one car! When choosing suppliers for rewards or the printing of vouchers and stickers, it's crucial to find one with a track record in this area. If partnering in a loyalty campaign is novel to a supplier as well as obviously lucrative, less scrupulous firms might seek to take advantage.

Returns: This is a risky business. That's why, in over 45 years in the industry, we've seen a number of our competitors go out of business. At the end of a major campaign, if poorly structured or executed, millions of euros' worth of stock often need to be taken back by us (or our competitors) and shipped to another market. As such, the harsh reality is the immediate need for cash in order to finance the huge amounts of stock to run the campaign and its eventual returns. We have the financial strength to do this. Some of our competitors less so. TCC has always worked tirelessly to mitigate these risks, with departments in every office around the world focused entirely on harnessing historical campaign data to provide accurate sales projections and forecasting. I wholeheartedly believe that's why, after 30 years, TCC is still in business.

It's also worth mentioning that, in the past, some of our big retail customers have tried to implement these campaigns on their own and ended up with full warehouses of stock, vowing 'never again'. On these occasions, we've been able to turn their negative experiences into a positive sales opportunity for our business, with their new-found respect for the true value of our historical data and 'no risk' returns guarantee. I repeat: this is a risky business! We're only here because we have learned our lessons from the past. Excess inventory is a direct result of inadequate sales projections, poorly structured campaigns and poor execution. We continue to hold true to our core beliefs and learn from every new campaign we run.

Excess inventory is a direct result of inadequate sales projections, poorly structured campaigns and poor execution.

Even with all the checks and balances of the four pillars, to some extent it remains a subjective process. One of the promotions we ran in Switzerland, offering a Guinness Book of Records-style collection of partworks, didn't do nearly as well as we'd imagined. We'd printed millions of books thinking it was going to be a great success. Sadly, a large number were not redeemed. This is why a solid returns strategy is a must. There are numerous businesses that specialise in buying up job lots of end of line goods to sell on at markets or discount retailers. These so-called jobbers can make a lucrative living out of such deals. However, while it might seem like an easy solution to get rid of excess rewards and close out the promotion, think the process through first. How will these jobbers be marketing your returns? Any customer that has doggedly collected points week after week to gain a coveted reward would be a little disappointed if they then came across the same reward being sold off cheaply elsewhere. This would also be the case if a retailer decided to sell off their excess rewards stock at a deep discount at the end of the promotion. At best the results of both scenarios would greatly diminish the pride shoppers had in their achievement. At worst, it would translate into anger at the retailer because the promotion wasn't quite as advertised. If a retailer has bulk bought goods on the understanding their brand would be part of an exclusive in-store rewards programme, there are also implications for the brand partner. Selling off the branded goods elsewhere at a deep discount could well be seen as diminishing its carefully honed image.

Strategic partnerships: Partnerships between companies with a similar demographic can work well for all parties. In fact, a good joint campaign can double the chances of success. Here, a retailer could work with, say, a national newspaper to give away a voucher in every paper. Readers can then take the voucher to the retailer to redeem the reward. It encourages individuals who normally shop at Retailer A to try Retailer B. The promotion can be run over a series of weeks, to help cement the habit. The retailer could, for example, give away an album on the first visit, for the newspaper readers to secure their collection of stickers. It's all about encouraging repeat behaviour.

The success of any loyalty campaign – to establish a deep and lasting bond between the customer and retailer – depends upon these four pillars. The shared goal and invitation to collect points towards rewards drive powerful human emotions and values such as status, achievement, nostalgia and a sense of belonging. When the gift is successfully collected, it further serves as a tangible reminder of a store's gesture of appreciation and respect, strengthening the relationship between shopper and retailer.

25. Know how to measure success

As with any marketing endeavour, there needs to be a way to measure the effectiveness of the campaign. What does success look like? While there's a clear aim to surprise and delight customers, it would be rare to find an organisation that doesn't seek to quantify the results. It can be a bit of a blunt instrument to judge success by comparing non-members to members. Not all members of a loyalty programme are equal. Some will begin to actively collect points but never redeem them, while others will enthusiastically throw themselves into the promotion and collect as many rewards as they can. While an active collector (but not a regular redeemer) will spend 10 per cent more than someone who has started to collect but not actively so, regular redeemers will spend 25 per cent more than inactive members (Carluccio et al 2021). The most obvious measure is ROI, which measures the benefits gained as a result of an investment (revenue) versus the costs. There are a few different ways to calculate this but at its simplest:

$$\text{ROI} = \frac{\text{Gain from investment - cost of investment}}{\text{Cost of investment}}$$

The difficulty lies in the fact that, compared to other promotion techniques and investments, calculating the gains versus costs of a loyalty programme can be more complex as they represent a longer-term investment with less immediately tangible benefits.

As with any marketing endeavour, there needs to be a way to measure the effectiveness of the campaign.

Loyalty programmes help retailers achieve a number of different business objectives, such as:

▶ customer loyalty (obviously)

▶ customer satisfaction

▶ customer retention

▶ sales

▶ brand awareness

▶ frequency

▶ basket size

▶ bringing alive a core strategy such as sustainability or fresh.

Therefore, to properly measure a campaign's effectiveness, a range of analytics may be required, according to the organisation and the type of campaign involved. Some of the most useful metrics are listed below:

Customer lifetime value: To work out the annual revenue per loyalty programme member, the following equation can be used:

Customer lifetime value =
(annual revenue per customer x customer relationship in years)
- customer acquisition cost

Customer retention rate: As the title suggests, this is a measure of how long a customer sticks with a retailer. The goal of a loyalty programme is to increase this number, which will in turn add to the bottom line. Even a percentage point increase can make a substantial difference. It has been calculated that a 5 per cent increase in customer retention can lead to a 25–100 per cent increase in profit.

Reduced churn: Customer churn is the rate at which customers leave a retailer to go elsewhere. Negative churn, where customers do the opposite, is therefore another important measure.

Purchase habits: If the programme's aim is to increase frequency of purchase of certain items such as fresh food, it will be easy to calculate via till receipts if this goal was successful.

Shift in attitude: Stores seeking to change customer perceptions will need to use research to find out if attitudes are changing. Online forums and social media mentions are hugely useful resources in this endeavour. What are customers saying about the store now? Is it positive? How much has it changed from before the campaign?

LOYALTY LEGENDS

Shoot for the stars: Conad, Italy

In 2021, after 10 years of running community campaigns to benefit local schools, Italian retailer Conad faced a challenge. The grocer, with a range of stores from neighbourhood to hypermarkets, wanted a significant promotion to celebrate a decade of helping children but the pressure was on to make it useful, authentic and with real educational value. Families and schools were still grappling with the impact of Covid-19, which had severely interrupted the education of millions of children.

Fortunately, Conad already had a successful model to build upon which had developed from its first community campaign that combined a collection of Smurf cards for kids with a giveaway of IT and educational equipment to elementary and secondary schools. In the ensuing years, the mechanism had evolved to include a more active involvement from the youngsters, with the launch of an annual writing contest. Children were encouraged to write a short story on a given theme such as healthy eating or friendship, and eight of the winning stories were published in books that could be collected in-store by Conad shoppers. Also on offer in each campaign were vouchers that could be redeemed for essential school equipment, as well as personal rewards to shoppers to encourage them to take part in collecting vouchers.

The annual Conad schools campaign has grown in popularity each year and more than four million books are now given away in each year's promotion. It's become an important part of the school calendar, beginning with the launch of the contest in September, along with a giveaway of the materials required, moving onto the judging and then the launch of the books in the summer months. Each campaign is supported with online resources for teachers, which can be downloaded and used in lessons, as well as a dedicated website. It is, of course, crucial to engage teachers since they both deliver the educational message and encourage children to write stories.

Conad always works with partners from relevant organisations, from the World Wildlife Fund (WWF) to Disney. As well as providing essential resources, representatives of partner organisations tour schools to build upon the themes and encourage participation.

The partners for the 2021 campaign added a real layer of excitement: the European Space Agency (ESA) and Italian Space Agency (ASI). Space almost universally captures the imagination and interest of children. Exploring the subject helps them understand their place in the universe and sparks curiosity, encouraging children to become creative thinkers. Building a campaign around space was the perfect way to enthuse children jaded by too much time away from school and make STEM (science, technology, engineering and mathematics) more appealing.

To add another layer of fun to Conad's space-themed campaign, a collection of Hey Clay space monsters were created, along with instructions for how kids could make their own versions. Students were invited to write their own short story along a STEM theme and 12 winning stories were published in a glossy Story Spaziali book. As always, participating schools were also able to collect and redeem vouchers for educational and IT equipment.

Despite many schools still being in lockdown, more than 22,000 enrolled in the campaign and more than 100,000 project materials were downloaded. Conad shops distributed 45 million clay sachets to kids so they could mould their own space monsters. As a result of the promotion, schools received more than €3 million of free equipment. Overall, 84 per cent of Conad shoppers said their perception of the retailer had improved thanks to the campaign.

6 LESSONS ABOUT THE CAMPAIGN LAUNCH

26. Create noise and excitement

Picture the scene. A woman approaches a store. She doesn't always shop here but it's convenient, falling on the route between work and home, and can always be relied on to offer a decent selection of fresh food. As she approaches the full-height glass panes of the automatic front door, the woman notices a tall banner dominated by a simple question: Are you collecting? Below this, there's a quirky photo of a girl posing with an odd sort of hat on her head. (On closer inspection, the hat turns out to be a frying pan.) Beneath this is an invitation to collect points to build up a collection of branded Italian cookware. It's a good brand, too – known for being the best quality. The bottom portion of the poster features a strip dominated by just one word, FREE, picked out in white letters on a bright red background.

If the message hasn't hit home, that's not a problem. While she's picking out her salad and vegetables, she couldn't fail to notice shelf edge tickets repeating the same question: Are you collecting? The tickets are interspersed with others that declare: FREE, 14 cm saucepan when you collect 20 points. When she looks up, she sees that attached to each end of the aisle is a large bunch of balloons celebrating the new rewards promotion: Are you collecting? By the time the customer heads out of the fresh foods section, she can't have failed to notice the event. Even if by any small chance she has, she can't ignore the new free-standing unit that has appeared at the end of the aisle. It's stacked, floor to ceiling, with every pot

111

and pan available in the Italian cookware collection, along with a reminder to make sure to pick up points at the cash desk. Spend €20 to receive one point. Are you collecting?

Everywhere this customer looks as she wheels her trolley around the store, there are banners and flyers urging her to get involved. Occasionally, the store's public address system will come to life, reminding customers to pick up their points at the till. There's a fun, almost carnival atmosphere in the shop. This is confirmed when the customer reaches the till and the cashier smiles broadly and hands her the points she's earned from her shop.

'Two more shops like this and you'll get the saucepan,' the cashier reminds her. 'Have you seen them? I've collected two myself so far...'

'Are you collecting?'

Creating noise and excitement around a rewards campaign is essential.

Creating noise and excitement around a rewards campaign is essential. Plenty of organisations see the value in rewarding their best customers and coaxing good customers to become better ones. However, 65 per cent of consumers engage with less than half of the loyalty programmes to which they're exposed (Morgan 2020). Once a retailer has defined the rewards it's going to offer, and refined elements of its campaign such as the spend, duration and other logistics, execution is key. The success, or otherwise, of any campaign depends upon how the benefits are communicated to the customer and 'lived' by the stores that offer them. If the campaign launch goes badly, it's almost impossible to recover from it and it will make everything that has gone before a waste of time. Or, as one of my colleagues will often say, 'It takes as much time and effort to run a bad programme as a good one. Don't miss the bus.' A number of elements need to come together to ensure a campaign's success. The process begins before the promotion is revealed in-store with a significant launch event designed to inspire the whole in-store team, from managers through to frontline staff, so they fully get behind the promotion and give it the momentum it needs from the off. Getting everyone together ahead of a promotion ensures nothing is left to chance.

27. Get the store manager on side and create a great launch event

The role of individual store managers in the success of a promotion cannot be underestimated. They are key to getting everyone behind it. Our own research shows that individual stores that don't manage to get their teams fully behind loyalty campaigns experience participation levels 20 per cent lower than those that do. That's a significant amount over a 16-week campaign and, of course, substantially weakens the goal of increasing basket size and purchasing frequency. It is, of course, the store manager's role to make sure everyone is fully behind a rewards programme.

Individual stores that don't manage to get their teams fully behind loyalty campaigns experience participation levels 20 per cent lower than those that do.

If a store manager has previous experience of a loyalty promotion, they will get it. In fact, they'll welcome news of any forthcoming campaign and look forward to it almost as much as their customers. If they haven't previously participated in one, they may well be reluctant. When they're already time poor, launching and then running an intensive 16-week campaign might sound like a lot of

113

extra work. This is why launch meetings are so important. This is the opportunity to rev up store managers, both the converted and the soon to be converted, to get them excited about what's about to happen in their stores. They will, in turn, relay the exciting news to their in-store team who will play an essential role in the coming weeks. In-store teams will not only help direct customers towards the points collections and answer any questions; they're also charged with creating the carnival atmosphere that will make the urge to collect irresistible.

The launch event should be held no more than two weeks before the loyalty campaign arrives in stores. Generally, events like this can be held in any large theatre, hotel or sporting arena and representatives from each store involved in the campaign should be invited. I accept that this wasn't an option during the pandemic but prior to that, if there were no signs of such an event taking place, it wasn't unusual for us to call retail CEOs to tell them to get going! The occasion can also be videoed to show those back at the store who may not have been able to attend.

The important points to get across at the launch event are: why are we doing this and how are we doing it? It works best if the senior leadership team are involved because they can make it clear what they expect from everyone. This is what you can do to make it a success. This requires outlining the mechanics of the promotion, along with specific and achievable goals, such as:

▶ number of customer sign-ups

▶ increased number of transactions per customer

▶ increased units per transaction

▶ increased annual customer value.

While sharing goals indicates a serious side, the tone of such events should never just be all about the numbers. The idea is to create an interesting, exciting and engaging forum that gets everyone on board because they can see that the campaign will work well for everyone. The resulting sales uplift might, for example, have a positive impact on their annual bonuses or help individual stores reach targets more easily. The event should be dynamic, almost like a piece of theatre. Group exercises and active audience participation are great for encouraging individual stores to be creative and even a little competitive with one another. Managers and cashiers can brainstorm ideas such as individual in-store competitions that reward checkout operators for their part in the promotion. (As an aside, each year TCC rewards the team that makes the most of a programme with the Jeff Langton Award for Attitude. It was launched in honour of our merchandiser, who practically lived in stores, travelling across the country to make sure programmes were perfectly executed.) Plenty of inspiring video material should be on hand to show store teams how promotions looked in similar stores and how they were received by customers.

Group exercises and active audience participation are great for encouraging individual stores to be creative and even a little competitive with one another.

28. Understand the four golden rules of the promotion

Overall, the key takeaway from any launch event is to ensure everyone understands the four golden rules of the promotion:

Rule number 1: Make the campaign an event in-store. Everyone has a part to play in creating that carnival atmosphere.

Make the campaign an event in-store. Everyone has a part to play in creating that carnival atmosphere.

Rule number 2: Train your people so that everyone feels involved. The message must be clearly passed on to any member of the team who didn't attend the launch event.

Rule number 3: Cashiers should not ask customers if they want points. They should congratulate each one and hand their tokens to them.

Rule number 4: Daily reporting must be accurate and timely. This is crucial for managing stock and ensuring that adequate supplies of rewards flow to the store and demand is met. Similarly, it ensures that stores never receive too much stock. This can clog up stockrooms and may need to be returned, which adds to the costs of the scheme.

There was tremendous enthusiasm both from our associates and from our customers on the professional cookware continuity programme. I really have to attribute a lot of it to the very beginning when we rolled out this programme. We had a spectacular launch with all of the store directors and the front-end managers. Everybody understood it and there were incentives too. They all walked out of there with the energy and understanding of what we were trying to get done and how it was going to drive positive sales. Associate engagement is so important and getting everybody engaged and helping them understand what the programme was all about and what kind of rewards they could get was critical to the success.

Bart Bohlen, SVP sales and marketing, Albertsons

To better illustrate what's involved in a launch event, here's an example from Chicago-based supermarket chain Jewel-Osco, which ran a 16-week campaign rewarding shoppers with branded cookware in return for points. Exactly two weeks before the promotion hit the stores, more than 500 store managers and cashiers were invited to a large theatre in the centre of Chicago. Each one was slightly mystified to be given a large white chef's hat on arrival but the atmosphere was relaxed and pleasant, so they all played along. Many of the people there had worked at the chain for 30 years or more but had never met their colleagues from other stores.

From the moment everyone was ushered into their seats, it was clear that the theme of the event was ice hockey, a hugely popular sport in the region. The professional compere who kicked off the proceedings was dressed in the uniform of an ice hockey coach. She introduced the event in front of a large banner declaring: 'One goal'. She ramped up the excitement about what that 'one goal' might be to fever pitch, then declared that they were all there that day to share in 'one of the most exciting campaigns' Jewel-Osco had ever run. 'There is one reason to have you here today,' she announced, 'and that is to unite around one single goal: to raise our sales by 5 per cent.'

The 'coach' built on the ice hockey theme, announcing that the cookware giveaway would be a 'game changer' in the 'upcoming season'. A comic interlude was provided by two senior Jewel-Osco executives who were planted to heckle from the crowd. 'Wait a minute, coach, this stuff doesn't work.' To whoops from the audience of retailers, they were pulled onto the stage and sent off for 'time out'. With everyone warmed up and responsive to the message, the stage was handed over to other speakers who filled in the essential information, including the following:

▶ the behavioural changes anticipated from loyalty programmes and how they would lead to bigger baskets, more trips and ultimately that 5 per cent sales lift

- ▶ further details around the numbers, such as the intention to realise a 10–15 per cent increase in the number of shoppers who spend over $100 per visit
- ▶ information about the points collection process plus the number of points required per reward.

To drive the message home and make sure everyone was focused, the teams were invited to quickfire quizzes based on the figures: 'If a customer spends $39.20, how many tokens should you give out?'

Before the event closed with its grand finale, with a guest appearance by a much-revered hockey player, the compere outlined the four golden rules. In this case, the crucial in-store elements that were the key to winning were called 'plays', in keeping with the sporting theme:

Play number 1: Make it an event.

Play number 2: Train your people.

Play number 3: Don't ask customers if they want points; congratulate each one and hand their tokens to them.

Play number 4: Daily reporting must be accurate and timely.

By this time, every participant was fired up and excited about the forthcoming promotion. The final step was to give each one there a piece of cookware to take home. It's always nice to have a free gift but this one would ensure that the promotion stayed top of mind.

Did the Jewel-Osco team 'win'? Well, here are the scores: a sales lift of 4.7 per cent was achieved over the course of the promotion with a 47 per cent participation level. It was a pretty respectable performance in anyone's book and a lot of that success was down to the powerful launch event.

29. Never underestimate the power of human contact

Today, most retail chains offer a mixture of self-service and staffed checkouts. As you might observe, staffed checkouts are still in great demand even though they can be a significantly slower option. Self-service tills have been around for a while and are easy to use, even for the most ardent technophobe, but many shoppers are prepared to put themselves to the inconvenience of a few minutes' queuing because they value human contact. When it comes to the success of loyalty campaigns, the power of human contact cannot be underestimated – and this is why checkout operators play such a key role. They are the main point of contact between customers and the retailer and play so much more of a part than simply handing over points with a receipt. They're in pole position to make sure the customer is truly engaged in what's happening.

> *When it comes to the success of loyalty campaigns, the power of human contact cannot be underestimated – and this is why checkout operators play such a key role.*

Handing customers points with a message of congratulations is the perfect starter for a till-side conversation. If a customer is unsure or hesitant, it's an opportunity to create enthusiasm about the rewards on offer. It helps if cashiers are well versed in talking points around the sign-up process through to how customers can earn and spend rewards. In addition, checkout operators can answer any queries about the process, such as:

▶ How do I earn points?

▶ Do my points ever expire?

▶ How do the status tiers work? (If applicable.)

▶ Can I lose a status that I have earned?

If customers are confused about any of the finer details of how the programme works, cashiers will be able to help. It's also worth noting that stores shouldn't miss the opportunity offered by self-service tills. The machines should always be programmed to remind shoppers about the loyalty programme and encourage their participation.

Also, as outlined earlier, the role of store managers in maintaining the momentum is invaluable. As well as making sure that everyone is focused on the campaign, they can also foster an element of competition between stores. League tables of how individual stores fare against rival local stores should be prominently displayed in staff areas. These will act as a constant reminder to every team member to give it their all when they walk onto the shop floor. We've learned that a top-performing store manager can outperform a bottom-placed store by more than ten times. Such is the effect of a committed store manager.

LOYALTY LEGENDS

Making a buzz online: Unbeelievables, Delhaize, Belgium

The global bee population is in decline but we do have the power to act. A campaign by Belgian supermarket Delhaize, called Unbeelievables, focused on creating a buzz about bees to get everyone thinking about what they can do to protect bees as well as the planet. To kick things off, Delhaize offered a range of six plush soft toy rewards in exchange for points. (The plush used for the range of six bees was rather special, too. It was awarded a Green Product Mark for its use of 96 per cent recycled content, making TCC the first company in the world to receive such a mark for a toy product.) Also on offer was a sticker and album collection filled with useful facts about bees and how helping to protect them makes a huge difference to us all. The stickers could be scanned and came to life with more bee facts and educational content, as well as a series of games to really engage a new generation of bee lovers. What really got shoppers talking, though, was the accompanying giveaway of seeds, which came with a simple request: create a bee-friendly garden. In a short space of time, countless families were using what space they could to plant flowers and flowering plants that bees loved. Everyone was eager to share their efforts on social media, creating a growing sense of solidarity and community among those keen to raise awareness of the plight of bees. The multimedia campaign went on to engage 50 per cent of households in the country. That's quite a buzz for bees.

7 LESSONS FROM 40 YEARS IN THE BUSINESS

30. Evolve, evolve, evolve

Like any milestone birthday, TCC's 30th anniversary (which also meant over 40 years in the business for me) was a time for reflection. We'd started out with the comparatively simple goal to build stronger connections between retailers and customers and create a company we were proud of. A lot has changed since that time, both for us as a business and in the wider world. Many of the changes are cyclical, part of the natural ebb and flow of business. Sometimes, some strategies are flavour of the month or year and at other times they're not. We'd put the general response to loyalty programmes in that category. When TCC launched, branding was not really much of a thing. The majority of the rewards given away were made-up brands, exclusive ranges that we'd created by ourselves. Fast-forward a decade or so and the wider market became flooded with major brand names. By implication, to succeed, shopper rewards needed to be much-coveted labels such as Alessi, Grundig or Zyliss. If retailers didn't offer these brands in their rewards programmes, it's possible that their competitors would and that's what would capture the imagination of shoppers.

Interestingly, the story of brands has moved on again in recent years. We haven't quite gone full circle back to a stage where they're no longer a significant driver but there are signs that things have begun to cycle away from the perhaps two-dimensional perception that brands are the accepted shorthand for 'good quality' or 'best'. Some shoppers, and Generation Z in particular, are rejecting the perceived commercialism of a lot of well-known products and won't simply buy big labels because they are, well, big labels. With so much to choose from, both in physical stores and online, shopping (and loyalty) decisions about products are based on a wider range of criteria from price and sustainability to recommendations on social media. Trust in big institutions is on the decline, no matter how much they spend on marketing and promotion.

In loyalty terms, it's early days for this trend. There are certainly plenty of older shoppers who still place a great deal of value on brands. We also don't believe that we will see a complete return to where we've come from. Things will just be a little different. Big brands are already moving to accommodate the shift in public sentiment. Many of the rewards now on offer still carry big brand labels but have been reformulated to reflect new appetites by increasing the use of recycled and environmentally friendly materials.

Where we have seen a complete and lasting change over our three decades is thanks to digital. The internet has changed the general outlook considerably and not just because consumers can now shop in a seemingly endless variety of locations, both physical and digital. Retailers are no longer simply competing against other retailers for a share of everyone's attention. It's now the norm for people to spend hours on their phones and other digital media each week, meaning there's so much more vying for our precious time. With access to so many more channels, the general public has become more savvy too. They recognise and dislike anything that smacks of 'selling them' something, which translates into an increasing ambivalence to promotions and sales communications. For retailers to stay relevant and properly engage with customers, they must cut through a lot more noise.

Many of these digitally led changes have been accelerated by the pandemic. Repeated lockdowns signalled an abrupt full stop to previous habits and loyalties. People became more 'homely' after extended periods at home with their families and rediscovered the simple pleasures of cooking and eating meals together.

We have yet to see how this will play out in the medium to long term but it doesn't make business sense to wait and see. For all retailers, a meaningful loyalty programme is an important part of a targeted strategy to keep customers coming back and spending more. At the same time, campaigns need to keep changing and evolving to reflect the altered outlook of the shoppers that retailers want to engage.

Campaigns need to keep changing and evolving to reflect the altered outlook of the shoppers that retailers want to engage.

As this book has shown, loyalty is nothing new. The majority of companies currently run some sort of customer engagement or loyalty programme (Morgan 2020). In the aftermath of the pandemic, nearly 72 per cent of businesses with an existing programme were planning an overhaul of what they'd been doing to make a bigger impact (Antavo 2022). Retailers are actively considering the priorities of shoppers today and exploring how loyalty programmes can evolve in line with their changing expectations. The goal is, of course, to keep things from becoming stale. There's no such thing as a finished loyalty strategy. Campaigns need to be consistently innovative to stand out from what's being offered by competitors.

It's absolutely key to support and reinforce a retailer's strategy, particularly in fresh or food waste/sustainability – making the brand of the supermarket the hero, not the brand of the reward.

The most effective way to achieve this is to tackle it from two angles:

The mechanics of the loyalty programme: Thanks to the digital revolution there are a variety of new and interesting ways to engage with customers and to encourage them to try something new. It is, however, when digital is combined with physical marketing that programmes can really fly.

Customer experience: Customers still enjoy gifts, points and rewards but are increasingly looking for retailers to offer promotions that align with their interests and personal values. Today's rewards need to fully resonate with their beliefs and concerns over sustainability and resources.

31. Blend the physical and the digital

Back in the 1970s, 20 years before TCC started out, the average person could expect to see between 500 and 1,600 adverts a day via a combination of TV, billboards and newspapers. Today, thanks to digital marketing, the average person is exposed to between 6,000 and 10,000 advertising messages in the same 24-hour window (Carr 2021). Not surprisingly, we're all pretty jaded by it all. Some people are so fed up with it that they actively shun as many of these promotions as they can via ad blockers. Even those that grudgingly put up with them are usually fairly apathetic about what's on offer.

Where, then, does this leave loyalty? Most retailers agree that customer experience is what will decide the winners and losers in the world of shopping. To get out in front and stay there, stores need to build relationships with customers and repeatedly drive home the message that they are there for them and listening to what they want. Not only that but they also need to show that shopping can be a fun, engaging experience. The most powerful way to do this is to blend physical, virtual and community experiences into each customer's

Wellcome Hong Kong's highly successful Kappa luggage campaign

journey. In omnichannel campaigns (see lesson 33), each medium will have its part to play. Digital has the power to create that all-important awareness away from a store. It offers a crowd-pleasing degree of flexibility, allowing customers to choose how, where and when they interact with retailers. Meanwhile, the physical engages shoppers once they walk through the doors and drives their spend behaviour. Together, the mediums create multiple touchpoints to lead shoppers towards the end goal, which is of course customer loyalty.

Customer data is key here. Blending the digital/physical experience helps retailers understand more about shopper behaviour out of store. The insights gained from when customers engage in a virtual world can be used to deliver tailored experiences in stores. Similarly, in an integrated loyalty programme, retailers understand more about shopper behaviour, such as how they interact with retailers out of store and what content they view, click and share.

Blending the digital/physical experience helps retailers understand more about shopper behaviour out of store.

Joined-up physical and digital campaigns are increasingly the norm and many retailers are becoming highly creative. Well-run omnichannel campaigns will have a noticeable impact on the bottom line too. Starbucks' rewards programme, which launched in 2008, now has more than 25 million members and generates nearly 50 per cent of the coffee giant's revenue (Starbucks 2021). Customers download the Starbucks Rewards app to get started and thereafter earn 'stars' for each purchase. They can also participate in online games to earn additional stars. Members can use the app to order ahead and pay, and stars can be exchanged for free refills, add-ons, food and drink items. The mechanic has a tier system, which offers better rewards the more stars are collected. Fifty stars, for example, will earn the user a free hot coffee, tea or croissant, while 200 earns food items such as a protein box, salad or a sandwich. Every part of the promotion is targeted towards encouraging members to walk past competing outlets and prioritise a visit to Starbucks. And it clearly works.

Getting the balance right between digital and physical is key. Not everyone has grown up with a mobile phone in their hands. Physical games such as scratch cards still hold a huge appeal to those who are more familiar with the pre-digital concept. Also, it would be wrong to ignore the tactile pleasure to be had from completing a full card of stickers or tokens. It's a pleasure that still resonates with all age groups. Indeed, when we have run physical and digital promotions in tandem, there is plenty of evidence to show that physical can still be more popular than digital, particularly in locations where smartphone usage is still low. This is reflected in surveys that show 39 per cent of consumers who participate in promotions still like to play physical scratch cards, against 28 per cent who say they prefer to play digitally. In the middle ground of the two camps, 33 per cent are happy to play in either medium (Sight-X 2021).

In a world where we now get so much for free, a physical gift can often seem even more generous.

You also can't forget that people have grown accustomed to not paying for online content. Most organisations give away vast amounts of information online, which they use to build their profile and credibility. The majority of newspapers and magazines post acres of free content and around five billion videos are watched on YouTube each day (Cook 2022), with 30,000 hours of content being added every hour (Ceci 2023). Much of this is valuable and useful but the abundance of it does diminish the wow factor. It's another reason why we strongly believe there's still an important role for physical to play in the loyalty space. Indeed, in a world where we now get so much for free, a physical gift can often seem even more generous.

Perhaps the most important criterion integral to the success of any campaign that combines a mixture of digital and physical is this: each of the activities involved should be fun. Customers don't care about how well a retailer is putting their own brand message across. If any of the elements are not well designed, they won't engage. Put a smile on a customer's face and you'll already be well on the way to creating a lasting bond.

32. Get in on gamification

I've talked a lot about in-store mechanics and physical promotions, so it might be helpful to look more closely at the latest development in the digital world. Remember, though, that this is not an and/or. Digital campaigns are there to complement in-store activity.

When it comes to loyalty, one of the most effective uses of digital is gamification. Why? Well, game playing isn't just for kids. Gamification creates a positive bond with shoppers of all ages because the mechanics of gameplay such as competition, ranking and scoring systems tap into our enduring instinct to want to play and celebrate our achievements. If the game is free to play, so much the better. The prospect of getting something for little or no effort gives you a natural high. But there's more to it than that. It often encourages you to feel special that you even qualified for this gift at all. Even though the rational side of your brain might know this online offer is open to all, there will be a big part of you that feels you earned the freebie. Then, once your ego is thoroughly massaged, you feel good about the brands that offered you this opportunity to prove your worth. You trust them to do the right thing. This positive impression encourages you to want to return the favour by doing business with the retailer that engaged you.

Digital gamification delivers huge opportunities for engagement

Gamification creates a positive bond with shoppers of all ages because the mechanics of gameplay such as competition, ranking and scoring systems tap into our enduring instinct to want to play and celebrate our achievements.

These emotions are hard to ignore: 64 per cent of shoppers said they'd 'like a retailer more' if they won something in a game. It translates into action, with 52 per cent saying they'd 'like a retailer and would buy from them' if they won something for free (Sight-X 2021), and our own survey shows 70 per cent of redeemers go to stores within 24 hours of winning a prize. Once they're in-store to collect their prize, 97 per cent followed through by buying goods (Spar SA 2021). The rule of reciprocation plays a part too since we hate to feel indebted to others and are therefore keen to settle up. Retailers benefit from the halo effect around the joy of winning an online game and that provokes action.

The strong emotional connection derived from a good online game makes you more inclined to recommend a brand to your loved ones. Our surveys show that 30 per cent of shoppers who engage with digital gamification come from word of mouth recommendations. A good friend or member of their family excited by receiving something free has said, 'You must try this.' What this translates into is a high demand for loyalty campaigns that include at least some element of gamification. Sight-X surveys show that 79 per cent of shoppers like to play for a chance to win prizes and 70 per cent engage at least once a month in these campaigns. Most of all, games are a great way to build relationships with customers and subsequently influence their decision-making process about where to shop. Today, from our own research, 55 per cent of those that participate in loyalty programmes join in after seeing, and indeed playing, games online and are therefore fully aware of campaigns before they visit stores. Quick and simple chance-based games with instant win mechanics are key to driving bursts of excitement and engagement. There's also a balance to be struck between mapping into micro moments within the shopper's day to reward them for engagement versus delivering longer, more complex skill games that engage more niche customers but may not appeal to the masses.

Instant win scratchcards continue to excite and reward shoppers

Quick and simple chance-based games with instant win mechanics are key to driving bursts of excitement and engagement.

Interest in games and gaming is enduring too. Our own research shows that over an eight-week campaign period, shoppers play an online game an average of 10 times. It's available 24/7 too, offering everyone a chance to play at least once a day. Once shoppers get used to the idea, they will return day after day for another chance. Did I win today? Our data from digital campaigns often shows customers logging in at a minute past midnight, or a spike in activity at 7 am when people first wake up.

One of the most striking examples of how engaged people can become came via a game we ran with a Danish supermarket. Our subsidiary, Gametation, uses a 'heat map' that monitors how many people are playing a game at any given time. As might be expected, this heat map showed a steady network of players from all over Denmark. One day, though, a player appeared in the Seychelles, 7,760 km away. This individual was clearly away on holiday but had become engaged enough with the game to see if they'd won anything that day. Upon closer scrutiny, it emerged that players were popping up all over the world, repeatedly checking in with the game.

There's a serious point to be made here too. There's a vast quantity of data that can be collected from even the most simple campaigns, offering key insights into shopper behaviour such as:

▶ how/when/where customers engage with games

▶ how they redeem their prizes

▶ whether they choose to redeem some prizes over others.

Each answer can help shape future campaigns to make them more successful.

Another obvious tick in the box for digital is that it's the medium of choice for Generation Z, the first to be brought up surrounded by technology. This group has now overtaken millennials and baby boomers to become the largest consumer group, accounting for 40 per cent of global consumers. In the US alone, their spending is worth an estimated $150 billion to the economy each year (McConnell 2021). As every marketeer will know, this group is notoriously difficult to reach, partly due to their notoriously brief attention span. Digital, and in particular gamification, is therefore the perfect link to an in-store campaign, since it offers enjoyable, bite-sized content.

However, the power of digital doesn't end when a customer walks through the door of a store. There are so many more opportunities to grab and hold the interest of customers. Think here of the following:

Easy accessibility: Combining physical and digital adds another layer of ease when it comes to accessing loyalty rewards. One of the most obvious mechanics is to encourage shoppers to use apps as a digital means to record rewards, badges and points on personal devices. Omnichannel can also reduce any sign-up friction when joining the programme.

Badges: Interest in rewards campaigns can be increased with in-app badges for reaching certain collecting milestones. Shoppers love achieving these goals and being recognised for them. The visual representation of a badge reinforces the feeling of accomplishment.

Competitions: In-app competitions that are closely tied with live, in-store events are a great way to expand the immediate excitement around a promotion.

Leagues and scoreboards: Online leagues and points collecting scoreboards build on the community feel of campaigns. Shoppers will begin to compete against one another and in doing so will feel closer to one another.

Personal best: Everyone likes a challenge and including a mechanic to measure their own performance against their previous best score encourages them to come back for more.

33. Omnichannel is becoming omnipotent

In days gone by, news about rewards collections was mainly spread by word of mouth. Families and friends would get together to discuss promotions and swap rewards and points. Today, of course, there's a plethora of different digital means to communicate and each one has had an impact on the loyalty business. Thanks to social media, our collecting communities have grown and spread out geographically. Customers can and do go online to ask others to help them build up loyalty points towards desired items or for help collecting specific pieces to complete a set. It's not unusual to see dedicated pages for like-minded collectors. It makes sense to ease the way for collectors to find one another, helping to manage a community that encourages customer to customer interactions. Retailers running loyalty promotions should always flag them on their own online channels. As well as giving customers access to essential information, they can also encourage discussion on Facebook and Instagram.

While it used to be the case that people would trust their peers more than anyone else, we are now just as, if not considerably more likely, to turn to influencers, Instagram stars, Twitter personalities and YouTubers for advice and recommendations. In fact, four out of 10 millennials say their favourite influencer understands them better than their friends (Digital Marketing Institute 2021). It's not just the younger generation, either; more than half of all women make purchasing decisions based on influencer posts. That sort of reach can't be ignored. It was certainly what motivated us to invite an influencer to talk to some of the team at TCC so much of what she said struck home. This particular woman blogged, tweeted and posted about her experience of being a mum and was followed by others like her from all over the world. That's a tightly defined audience of like-minded people. For any retailer seeking to strike a chord with mums, this is surely the best place to start. Working with an influencer is far more effective than adverts in a newspaper or on TV, which go to everyone. (Not to mention their readership/viewership has a fraction of the reach.) So much of their role has been replaced by influencers, who often have the ear of millions of people.

Working with an influencer is far more effective than adverts in a newspaper or on TV, which go to everyone.

The influence and enormous reach of celebrities from actors and musicians to athletes can't be ignored either. The world's most-followed person at the time of writing, Cristiano Ronaldo, has 552 million followers on Instagram. If the brand values are complementary, it can be a powerful way to engage a large number of individuals. This is why we partnered with supermodel Naomi Campbell on a rewards promotion that featured handbags, towels and luggage and many of our cookware promotions have been fronted by well-known chefs. In the past, we've worked with retailers to organise tie-ups with winners of MasterChef or TV chefs such as Gordon Ramsay and the late Keith Floyd. This strategy can be extended further by negotiating TV tie-ins. There are, after all, multiple TV channels today and thousands of hours of programming are needed to fill them.

There's a lovely story about Pelé (probably the most famous football star of all time), with whom we partnered in 2013. We ran a campaign in Tesco stores across central and eastern Europe, which included Pelé-branded footballs and various limited edition merchandise. While he was appearing at supermarkets and speaking at events (drawing huge crowds), we discovered that he'd become good pals with John Lennon after they'd met at the Berlitz Language School in New York. Lennon was studying Japanese and Pelé (who was playing for the New York Cosmos at the time) was working hard to improve his English.

I was in Holland attending our annual marketing showcase. Pelé had agreed to speak at our event and kindly made time for selfies with over 300 guests! I was staying at the Amsterdam Hilton – the hotel made famous by John Lennon and Yoko Ono's honeymoon 'bed-in' protest – and had been allocated the John & Yoko Suite, complete with memorabilia from their legendary stay back in 1969.

One of my colleagues had been presented with a limited edition John Lennon pen by Mont Blanc (the clip was in the form of a keyboard to celebrate the song 'Imagine'), so we decided to buy another one to give to Pelé in appreciation of his work with us. We thought it would be a special gesture to present the gift to him in the John & Yoko Suite.

We invited him to join us and he was both surprised and moved when he understood the historical significance of the room. My colleague and I presented him with his unique gift, which he was genuinely thrilled to receive. I have such fond recollections of that day, and I have photographs of us together in the suite that will always remind me what a funny, gentle, charming and humble man he was.

What this experience with Pelé taught me was the sheer power of celebrity. I saw colleagues go weak at the knees in his presence and he was mobbed wherever he went. Never before had I witnessed this level of the 'celebrity effect' and it was testimony to the impact that endorsements of this kind can have on a campaign. The Pelé programme went on, of course, to become a huge success.

Pelé with Richard Beattie in the John & Yoko Suite, Amsterdam Hilton

While finding the right celebrity to partner with a brand can considerably boost the message, celebrity endorsement/tie-ins don't come cheap. If budgets don't allow there are alternative options. It is, for example, possible to use online sites associated with a famous name. Thus if, say, a retailer runs a programme giving away Harry Potter merchandise supported by a themed smartphone game, it makes sense to flag the opportunity on relevant Harry Potter fan accounts on Instagram or TikTok. Experience has shown that it's possible to create up to a 500 per cent uplift in user engagement through thoughtful targeting of complementary media. For the best chance of connecting and engaging with customers, make sure the brand values of the influencer, celebrity or complementary social media channels are a good fit. Many of the rules in the next section on licensing and partnerships will apply here too.

34. Leverage character licensing – choose your partners carefully

It doesn't matter what age you are or how cynical you've become, the chances are that you'll still vividly remember the TV, movie or literary character that was the centre of your world as a child. Close your eyes and you'll be transported to the time you dressed up to look like them or imagined what you'd do if you had their superpowers. These powerful emotions echo down the generations; what changes are the characters. For this reason, character licensing is a strong force in loyalty programmes and remains one of the most effective ways to reach families with young children. In recent years, we've seen an increasing number of studios gravitate towards character licensing. Indeed, we've seen that many have now introduced their own loyalty reward strategies, something that would've been unheard of 10 years ago.

Licensing works so well because it transfers the positive emotions already generated around a TV or film franchise towards the brand championing the licensed product. Customers look at a display of familiar and much-loved characters and a bond is quickly established. For retailers with an international footprint, licensing can offer real value for money. Well-known characters have global appeal so it's possible and indeed cost effective to run campaigns across multiple locations. There's also the plus point that if a licensing deal coincides with a release of a new production featuring the character, the retail promotion benefits from the (usually) multimillion dollar marketing efforts of the studios.

Over the years, we've worked with a wide range of licensed characters from much-loved film franchises such as Star Wars to TV staples from Scooby Doo to Angry Birds. We've also licensed popular toy brands such as Nerf by Hasbro, which makes the phenomenally successful range of blaster guns and super soakers.

Since we're currently experiencing a surge in interest in licensing and partnerships, it might help to share a few of the key things that we've learned along the way.

Know your audience: It's easy to get carried away by characters that have significant brand recognition and conclude they'll offer greater potential for exposure than lesser-known figures. However, what matters most is the demographics of the customers being targeted. A more mature customer base, for example, may not be particularly moved by a popular cartoon character, even if it's the must-see series of the day among younger fans. There are, however, fewer concerns if the main target is families. Kids will gravitate towards their favourite characters from the big and small screens and parents will help them finish their collection to keep them happy.

Mix and match: While there's a huge attraction to licensed characters, it's not a good idea to use them with every loyalty promotion. A collection of, say, Looney Tunes plush toys will always be hugely popular but it doesn't say anything in particular about the retailer offering them as a reward. It's much more effective to mix licensed character campaigns with ones more closely built around the retailer's objectives. Thus, a store group seeking to boost its sustainability credentials might test the water with an offer on a range of big, branded characters and then move on to a promotion giving away recycled cookware as a reward.

It's much more effective to mix licensed character campaigns with ones more closely built around the retailer's objectives.

Working in partnership with another brand can also be a highly effective way to significantly increase the appeal of a promotion and offset the overall cost of the campaign. Imagine, for example, a grocer that's keen to burnish its healthy eating credentials with an omnichannel promotion featuring an online game together with an in-store promotion giving away cookware rewards for a set spend. Partnering with an organisation selling a range of additive-free juice drinks could increase the appeal of the promotion and help bring shoppers in-store. The healthy drinks company could be invited to advertise within the digital promotion as well as put up a number of instant-win prizes for the digital prize pool. This is great exposure for the drinks company because it will introduce their products to a whole new consumer group and encourage sampling. Meanwhile, these sort of instant-win prizes work well for retailers. Players who win a prize will be more inclined to stay longer in the digital game, clicking around the site to see what else is on offer. They will also need to go to the store to collect their juices, thus setting up the habit of shopping there.

Well-chosen partners can also add credibility to a campaign. In 2020, we partnered with the WWF, one of the world's largest independent conservation organisations, working alongside them on their mission to stop the degradation of the planet's natural environment and protect renewable resources. We undertook to raise funds and awareness for their conservation efforts and to promote sustainability through the 'For the Future' collection, a range of reduced plastic, co-branded sustainable products with low-impact packaging. We were confident that this partnership was taking us in the right direction but even we were surprised by the response from some of our retail partners. Reports came back that some major retailers were astonished that we were able to work hand in hand with the WWF on their sustainability strategies. Retailers want to be seen to be helping their customers' wellbeing and working with them to support their values. Adding the name WWF to the mix gave another layer of credibility, supporting their green credentials.

Ultimately, the market and the needs and desires of customers will continue to change and evolve over time. Constant research and observation are required to stay up to date with what's interesting and important to consumers and innovations may be required to meet their changing needs.

Constant research and observation are required to stay up to date with what's interesting and important to consumers.

LOYALTY LEGENDS

Guardians of the Earth: Lidl Portugal

With young Portuguese shoppers becoming increasingly environmentally conscious, Lidl Portugal decided a change of direction was in order. After many years of running promotions extolling the virtues of healthy eating, it switched to a campaign focused on raising its sustainability credentials. Guardioes da Terra, or Guardians of the Earth, centred around six likeable characters designed to highlight the various ways shoppers can get involved to help the planet protect its precious resources. The themes were chosen based on research indicating what most concerned consumers. Planet Earth is the teacher of all the Guardioes da Terra and has been helping them from an early age to use their powers for the good of the world, preserving and protecting the environment. This character loses strength whenever pollution increases. Planet Earth is joined by Solis, the wise man of the group who urges others to clean beaches. There's also Flora, the guardian of the forest; Flames, the sporty one who's dedicated to reducing energy consumption; Drops, who protects fish; and Bia, who's close to nature and prepares healthy and delicious meals for all the guardians.

Each character mirrors Lidl's own sustainable activities. Solis would, for example, be delighted with the plastic collections the retailer organises on beaches across Portugal in its TransforMAR project. Flames, on the other hand, will be keeping a close eye on Lidl's efforts to reduce in-store energy consumption with smarter heating and cooling equipment. Flora will certainly be impressed by Lidl's links with the Rainforest Alliance to ensure all bananas being sold in its shops have been grown sustainably.

Each of the characters was available to collect as a plush toy in a mug but their individual stories (and messages) were also built into the material that supported the campaign. Shoppers could also collect 120 cards featuring the Guardioes da Terra and a board game to go with them. This was further supported with a website and an app, where Guardioes fans could watch animations of the characters, read ebooks and play games.

More than 100 board games were distributed to primary schools to support the campaign and, during the promotion, a million Guardioes were redeemed. Lidl Portugal recorded a 90 per cent awareness of Guardioes, providing a real connection with environmentally focused shoppers, as well as an incremental sales rise of 2.6 per cent during the campaign.

8 LESSONS ABOUT THE RETAILER'S ROLE IN SOCIETY

35. Win customers' hearts and minds

Competition among retailers is always fierce as they fight to hold on to their best, highest-spending customers. Hard measures such as market share, average basket size, frequency of visits and customer retention continue to be key. However, to maintain or better still grow the numbers today, no retailer can afford to ignore the role they play in society. The message is simple: to get ahead and stay ahead, retailers need to appeal to customers' hearts and minds as well as their wallets.

To get ahead and stay ahead, retailers need to appeal to customers' hearts and minds as well as their wallets.

Even before the pandemic we were already seeing significant shifts in consumer behaviour and attitudes around the world. Thanks to the dogged efforts of campaigners, many millions have become sensitive to their own impact on the environment and started to reconsider personal consumption. Growing awareness of the origins of the goods we're buying translated into efforts to limit food waste, shop more consciously and choose more sustainable options. Attention has also turned to the impact our lifestyles have on wider society and the communities we live in. Rather than prior-

145

itising the convenience and time saving offered by big box and online retailers, individuals began to think more carefully about the pressures on the high street, prompting numerous campaigns to shop locally and support community stores. Meanwhile, healthy lifestyle messages have hit home, with a noticeable rise in plant-based diets and sales of fresh food.

As with so many things, Covid-19 accelerated these underlying trends. There's no doubt that consumers are now looking at the products they buy in an entirely new way. Large numbers are deeply unsettled about the prospects for the environment and the economy as well as their own health and communities, which means they're increasingly re-evaluating every aspect of their lives. Central to this is where, and how, we spend our money.

There are opportunities here for retailers, which have always been more nimble and flexible than state institutions. This customer-facing sector has a specific and well-practised expertise at connecting with individuals. Retailers have not been slow to react either. Not surprisingly, we've seen store groups everywhere adopt a greater degree of social responsibility. Corporate social responsibility (CSR) campaigns have, for some time, been the norm for every single retailer we've worked with around the world. These CSR campaigns are devoted to helping customers lead better, healthier lives and to improve the outlook for their communities.

What, though, does this mean for loyalty? Without a doubt the shift towards conscious consumption means that we need to move a long way away from the early continuity campaigns where points and rewards were the most effective way to secure customer engagement. The singular focus on the instant gratification to be had by gaining something for nothing has been significantly reduced. Today, 37 per cent of customers are motivated by rewards that don't seem to be connected to any sense of purpose (KPMG 2019). The majority of shoppers prioritise satisfying broader concerns on everything from product origin and trust and reputation around a brand to the health and safety of the people that work for it. This means that, to achieve the greatest impact, continuity campaigns now need to be about more than just product.

The future of loyalty lies in fully reflecting the beliefs and desires of shoppers. Customers show increased loyalty to stores that do things that resonate with their personal values. If a programme aligns with what's important to shoppers, retailers will forge a stronger emotional, value-based connection. This is what will encourage repeat visits.

The future of loyalty lies in fully reflecting the beliefs and desires of shoppers. Customers show increased loyalty to stores that do things that resonate with their personal values.

36. Design purpose-led campaigns

The goal of any loyalty programme remains to retain the best customers over the medium to long term. However, this needs to be in line with what's most important to shoppers right now. The priority for every retailer is to pinpoint what it is that motivates their customer base. What are the issues that keep them awake at night? What are the problems they most want to see solved? The answer to these questions will help guide retailers in designing initiatives that resonate with customers by helping them make a positive impact.

We know that consumers worldwide are concerned about a wide range of issues from the future of the planet and the influence of large corporations to what's happening in their own communities. Plus, as ever, families will prioritise the health and wellbeing of those closest to them. What concerns customers the most will also vary region by region. Retailers must do their own research to properly understand what impacts people in the area in which they operate. It's likely, however, that the most pertinent issues will fall into one of these three main categories:

1. Sustainability and the environment
2. Community and social
3. Health and wellness.

In the following sections, I'll look at each one in detail. I should, of course, add that there's no such thing as one size fits all and I recognise that each of these sections covers a broad category. In the area of sustainability, for example, the idea that there's only one type of sustainable shopper – the ubiquitous green warrior – would be totally wrong. While most people are conscious about the climate crisis and open to changing their shopping behaviours, opinions vary on the best course of action. Do we start by reducing the use of plastic, reducing CO2 or changing our diet? There are no unified answers and priorities vary from region to region. Again, it's up to individual retailers to make a judgement about what matters most to their shoppers.

37. Prioritise sustainability

Climate change is one of the biggest challenges of our time. We've all witnessed the result of years of inaction with extreme weather events, flooding, drought and rising sea levels. Scientists have warned that, if we continue to do nothing, there will be a dramatic impact on agricultural yields and many people could eventually be forced from their homes. There can be few people around the planet who aren't aware of the message from environmental experts that the time to act is now.

There has at least been some progress. For a measure of how far sustainability has exploded onto the agenda, look no further than how most major corporations address the subject today. For many years, any sort of environmental reporting was carried out at a high level and details about it were tucked away in the recesses of annual reports and accounts. Today, sustainability stats are prominently displayed front and centre on the websites of most organisations. In many instances, this is because sustainability has become an obligatory cost of doing business. Governments around the world are imposing strict environmental targets on companies under their jurisdiction and moves are already in progress to get in front of them. In Germany, for example, businesses are asking suppliers to commit to strict carbon reduction targets by 2030. If the suppliers do not comply, they won't retain their contracts.

There's another good reason why sustainability is now at the top of the agenda for corporations, over and above their statutory obligations: it's what their customers want to see. Across the world, 37 per cent of consumers say it's a very, or extremely, important factor in the choices they make when they buy goods (KPMG 2019). There are regional variations, though, with more than half of shoppers in China citing it as a real priority.

TCC prioritises sustainability and positive social impact

We're acutely aware that rewards have a great deal of environmental impact. How great that impact will be depends upon the choice of the raw material.

From TCC's point of view, as a continuity business we've had to adopt a very different message. If there's any perception that we are 'just a marketing company trying to push products on people' the message will be lost. Fortunately, we took the decision at least a decade ago to prioritise sustainability. This meant rethinking every aspect of our business. Take as an example the raw product used in our rewards. We're acutely aware that rewards have a great deal of environmental impact. How great that impact will be depends upon the choice of the raw material. Perhaps 60–70 per cent of the carbon footprint of a product comes from the raw material. When we can, we focus on choosing more environmentally friendly materials and recycled post-consumer materials. We've also moved away from loyalty rewards made from plastic. As ever, there's always more that can be done. TCC hired its first sustainability expert in 2020 and we now have an entire department dedicated to this hugely important area.

We continue to measure our environmental impact across everything we do and we communicate this crucial work through the business at every opportunity. We aim to use the same measurement methods as the retailers we work with, so we can match our customers' own objectives on the number of tonnes of recycled material being used, carbon emissions released and all the other variables being measured today. In the next ten years, we'd like to see all our products as sustainable, made using recycled and less environmentally damaging materials as well as more durable, so that they last longer. We're also keen to make sure we have a positive social impact in the factories that produce our products and that everything is clearly measured and transparent. Every single product should have the environmental labelling that we're already seeing on food products.

In January 2022, we joined the United Nations Global Compact (UNGC), a group of more than 9,000 companies working towards the same sustainable development goals. This made a lot of sense because most of our customers are already members of UNGC. To meet our UNGC obligations we have to measure any actions that might have a negative impact on the environment and society and set targets to improve our performance. There's an obligation to publicly communicate our progress on a yearly basis to all stake-holders, internal or external, holding ourselves accountable for what we do.

38. Think regeneration, recycling and repurposing

When weighing up future sustainable rewards initiatives, there are a number of options for solutions that also manage the risks to our environment and reduce the risks associated with climate change.

Regeneration, not offsetting: Mention sustainability and sooner or later you'll hear the words 'carbon offsetting'. The idea behind this is that planting trees to offset the carbon that's generated by the product itself will somehow make the problem go away. Logic dictates that tree planting may indeed offset the carbon generated but it doesn't solve the underlying issues. At best, it's simply putting a plaster on them.

Walmart was one of the retailers to speak out about carbon offsetting and move away from the practice by putting regener-ation on the agenda. Through its Project Gigaton, the American discounter has pledged to achieve zero emissions in its operations by 2040, none of which will be via carbon offsetting. One of the range of measures being implemented to achieve this goal is Walmart's work to help its suppliers adopt better farming practices such as cultivating heat-resistant crops.

How, we wondered, could these regenerative ideas work for loyalty programmes? Buoyed by Walmart's example, we began talking to some innovative start-ups and environmental entrepreneurs specialising in projects to help farmers to update and, where necessary, renew their equipment and production methods so there is less negative impact on the environment. Like Walmart, our goal is to tackle unsustainability right at the beginning of the supply chain. It's early days but we're already seeing some extremely innovative solutions. When we produce rewards from entirely sustainable resources, it provides retailers with a great opportunity to educate shoppers and demonstrate to them that, by purchasing goods to participate in a programme, they're actually having a positive impact on the environment at the same time.

Plastic recycling: Single-use plastics, from bottles to bags to food packaging, remain the most commonly discarded types of plastic. Made almost exclusively from fossil fuels, these throwaway items often finish their brief life cycle in landfill or the oceans. We've already seen that even the smallest shift in strategy by some of the world's major chains can have an impact at source. In 2021, UK supermarket group Tesco announced that it had succeeded in removing one billion pieces of plastic from its supply chain as part of its four-part environmental commitment on plastic. This was achieved through a range of measures. Hundreds of suppliers were informed that 'packaging would be a key part of its decision-making process' when it came to orders. Part of this initiative included a ban on deliveries shipped in plastic. Meanwhile, in-store, plastic-wrapped multipacks were banished, saving 67 million pieces of plastic each year.

We've already seen that even the smallest shift in strategy by some of the world's major chains can have an impact at source.

As well as reducing the amount of plastic we use, the goal is to recycle a large amount of the excess too to make robust, useful products, vastly increasing the material's shelf life. After all, plastic doesn't need to be a bad thing, as long as it can be kept in the consumption loop. Rewards programmes can play a role here, but again, it's early days.

Loyalty programmes require millions of rewards at a time, which makes it tough to immediately switch to offering goods solely made from recycled plastic. While the obvious retort is that the world is awash with plastic, just get on with recycling it, the truth is there are numerous issues in recycling plastic. Of the 8.3 billion tonnes of plastic produced worldwide, just 9 per cent has been recycled. The best (and quite optimistic) estimate is that we're managing to recycle 20 per cent of our plastic waste per year (Franklin-Wallis 2019).

Why are things moving so slowly? It's hard to believe now but much of the recycling technology we have today has only been available for a decade. Indeed, many methods were only at the university research level ten years ago and have yet to be scaled up to the size where they could be useful in factories. There are still large regional variations too. There are only a handful of factories in Europe that have the processes in place to recycle plastic on any scale. And for those seeking to use recycled plastic on anything that comes into contact with food, there's an extra layer of difficulty. Because of the risk of chemicals being released from the waste material, it's not possible to simply recycle plastic and then use the resulting product in direct contact with food.

This is why there's a raft of regulations in some regions that only permit the use of certified recycled material from fully audited recycling plants. However, progress is being made. We've already run a number of campaigns using rewards made from recycled plastic and a few are mentioned in this book. We expect to run many more in the future. It's a process we're prioritising because the demand is clearly there. As time goes on, we see recycled plastic taking centre stage as the focus of rewards promotions. After buying goods in plastic packaging, customers will be encouraged to return containers to reverse vending machines, in the knowledge that the waste will be recycled and made into rewards. Points will be earned for each item returned, which will go towards redeeming the recycled plastic rewards. It's a perfect, virtuous circle. The loyalty promotion is no longer just about the product – it introduces the idea of co-benefits and giving value to what used to be considered waste.

Reducing food waste: Between 2010 and 2016, food waste was responsible for 8–10 per cent of human-caused greenhouse gas emissions. Households in some western countries throw out up to one third of the food they buy (Plackett 2020), something the UN is keen to tackle with its sustainable development goals, which aim to halve food waste by 2030. Cooking food from scratch plays a key role in reducing food waste. Done well, it's far more efficient than buying ready meals when every household has different appetites. Supermarkets have done a lot to encourage this practice and, as we've already seen, rewards can play a role in this. A simple container can be crucial in helping consumers to organise their kitchens and store food more efficiently. Sets of high-quality kitchen knives make preparing food from scratch a pleasure, not a chore. Another useful category of rewards is homeware and bakeware. Owning a range of differently sized baking containers is also invaluable for controlling portion sizes. Households can collect points towards items that suit the size of their family.

We also need to recognise and support the return of a trend that has roots in past generations. In years gone by, our forefathers (or more likely foremothers) would cook a Sunday roast and then use the leftovers in a shepherd's pie the following day and perhaps in sandwiches the day after. Nothing would go to waste and, of course, it saved money. One of the advantages of cooking food from scratch is that it encourages us to do something similar today. A few hours in the kitchen can set up a household with meals for a number of days. Supermarkets can play a role in encouraging the repurposing of leftovers. As well as food containers, they can prioritise rewards such as hand blenders and mixers to whizz up ingredients and give them new life as a sauce or soup. We've already run a number of highly successful campaigns with MasterChef and Nutrifresh, offering rewards from their food preparation ranges.

Supermarkets can play a role in encouraging the repurposing of leftovers. As well as food containers, they can prioritise rewards such as hand blenders and mixers.

39. Beware greenwashing and wokewashing

Whenever there's a big shift in consumer trends, there are always unscrupulous companies that make grand statements about how they perfectly reflect the mood of the day. Websites will grandly declare that an organisation is fighting climate change/becoming 100 per cent sustainable/reducing waste, or all of the above. The messages will be repeated on packaging, adverts and signage throughout any physical premises. To drive the message home, declarations will often be accompanied by pictures of lush green landscapes.

To be fair, it's probable that many of the organisations that do this do mean well and genuinely care about the environment and sustain-

The Nutrifresh 'Free' programme in-store with supporting external advertising

ability. But if they don't walk the walk it can present real problems. Corporate honesty and transparency are crucial qualities that all age groups look for (49 per cent) and particularly so with millennials (51 per cent). In some regions such as Brazil and China, the desire for businesses to play fair is even higher, at 60 per cent (KPMG 2019). There's nothing more likely to turn off a customer than a campaign that smacks of 'greenwashing' or marketing spin that implies products are more environmentally sound or worthy than they really are. Shoppers are scrutinising every business they interact with to see if they reflect their beliefs. They are wary of anything that smacks of a 'social disguise', or campaigns that are 100 per cent focused on maximising profit. No one wants to feel manipulated and most consumers are savvy enough to recognise actions that benefit the company rather than address their concerns. If businesses don't get it right, individuals are more willing than ever to vote with their feet. They will change their buying behaviour if they don't approve of what a brand is doing. They're well aware that, in numbers, they have the power to create meaningful change.

It's increasingly difficult for any retailer and grocery stores in particular to dip below the radar or attempt to mask any half-hearted measures behind bold slogans. They will get called out in a very public way, either via social media or by campaign groups whose entire remit is to keep an eye out for greenwashing. Oxfam International's annual Supermarket Scorecard, for example, benchmarks chains worldwide on their performance in protecting people that produce the goods they sell. Stores are scored on four areas of transparency and accountability in their treatment of workers, small-scale farmers and women. Such 'name and shame' lists do have an impact. Stores that scored as low as 1 per cent in early lists have been prompted to engage with Oxfam and make commitments to improve in order to rise in the rankings.

When running any sort of promotion with a strong sustainable message, careful thought needs to be given to each element. Such programmes can be impactful when done effectively but they can be damaging if they're not. If, for example, the programme is high-lighting climate change and sustainability, the rewards themselves must have a reduced environmental footprint, no unnecessary packaging and ideally have some sort of recycling element. One of TCC's claims to fame is that we're one of the biggest purchasers of plush in the world (plush is the soft textile used for stuffed toys). Today, all of our plush is made out of recycled fabric and the same goes for the stuffing we use in toys. Another of our successes has been in luggage, where we've produced more than half a million pieces made from recycled plastic bottles. In the process, we have taken 25 million unwanted PET bottles out of the system.

No matter what the reward is in any campaign; it must reflect the overall message. If it doesn't, then maybe the message should be reframed. Promotions that miss the mark or appear in any way cynical will often provoke a wider backlash. There have, in the past, been howls of protest when 'junk food' brands have targeted schools via rewards programmes. Teachers' unions, advertising watchdogs and consumer groups have condemned schemes where children are encouraged to consume more crisps and chocolate in order to secure sports equipment or computers. The mismatch in the mechanic encourages unhealthy activity, which produces piles of additional plastic waste – and the reward is too great. The resulting furore can do damage to the brand and sales, significantly reducing or even destroying the impact of the loyalty programme itself.

No matter what the reward is in any campaign; it must reflect the overall message. If it doesn't, then maybe the message should be reframed. Promotions that miss the mark or appear in any way cynical will often provoke a wider backlash.

Retailers are uniquely placed to inspire people on a mass scale by reimagining campaigns and rewards to resolve issues such as food waste, recycling and protecting the planet. Just a few simple ideas can encourage more sustainable lifestyles and reinforce the right behaviours, which will benefit us all.

LOYALTY LEGENDS

Fighting the throwaway culture: Coop Italia

EU authorities have set a 2030 deadline for a ban on single-use plastics and microplastics but Coop Italia has pledged to beat that deadline by eight years. Beginning its campaign in 2018, Italy's second largest retailer and the leading seller of loose fresh fruit and vegetables from its 1,500 stores switched the packaging for 78 items in the fruit and veg range to recyclable or reusable, saving 960 tonnes of plastic. As its use of environmentally friendly packaging increases, Coop Italia forecasts that it will save 6,400 tonnes by 2025.

With such ambitious goals in place, it was vital that any promotions didn't just meet the pledge to use sustainable materials but also spread the message about the importance of protecting the environment. Meanwhile, any campaign had to work in partnership with Coop Italia's other core strategy: to support the local communities around each store. In 2019, Coop Italia launched its Re-Generation campaign to reinforce these messages with the slogan 'Good shopping can change the world'. The idea was to engage everyone in the community with a regeneration campaign that in particular focused on families, teachers and schools.

Re-Generation acted as the umbrella brand for a number of subsequent promotions. All rewards were to be either 'reborn' from existing product waste or from a certified sustainable production process. At the same time, an intensive campaign would run in parallel to explain to shoppers why this was so important. In the first year of Re-Generation, 25 million plastic bottles were recycled to become a collection of backpacks, laptop covers and bumbags that could be collected in-store. To help spread the word, Coop Italia worked with the Ministero Dell'Ambiente (Ministry of Environment) on its Coop per la Scuola message offering schools educational resources on the subject of protecting the environment, supported by a range of materials available for free on Coop's website. Shoppers could collect vouchers for dual rewards – a bag made from recycled material for themselves and points towards free equipment for local schools. More than 14,000 schools took part, redeeming more than 45,000 rewards worth in excess of €8 million.

The next stage of the Re-Generation promotion was launched in 2020. This campaign was in partnership with Italian kitchenware brand Guzzini, which produced an exclusive range of food containers made from more than 700 tons of recycled plastic. As well as maintaining the clear message about using recycled material, the campaign also had an additional purpose: discouraging food waste by providing the means to store leftovers. The attractive Guzzini containers were also perfect for packed lunches, creating another incentive. Once again, the campaign worked in partnership with schools, with a range of support material and free webinars focusing on the theme. In this case, there was an additional range of distance learning courses written in conjunction with Google and experts from the University of Florence. Coop Italia kept in touch with schools using a range of tools, including a direct email campaign, a dedicated website and app, social media, in-store point of sale materials and a call centre. The additional materials for this campaign proved to be a particularly useful resource for hard-pressed teachers since it ran throughout the pandemic when many schools were closed. Once again, a dual loyalty voucher was used for shopper rewards. Customers received one voucher for every €15 spent, with one half of the voucher redeemable for school materials from stationery to IT equipment and the other for the Guzzini storage products reward. This time, more than 21,000 schools enrolled, redeeming more than 53,000 rewards, valued at more than €10 million. When it came to Guzzini, Coop Italia experienced a 42 per cent redemption rate, with 3.2 million rewards collected. Analysis shows that Coop shoppers participating in the campaign spent 7 per cent more than those who did not.

The third Re-Generation campaign introduced a collection of Berndes gourmet cookware made from recycled aluminium and plastic and a recycled glass collection from Ugo Nespolo. Running alongside the offer under the slogan 'The rebirth of Italy' was a campaign designed to encourage everyone to support their local territory and economy. Among a range of initiatives, a well-known homegrown artist drummed up interest in a photo contest to capture the hidden wonders of the country. Once again, the Coop per la Scuola campaign for schools ran alongside all activity, building upon the work of previous years. Italy's teachers and headteachers were asked to describe Coop per la Scuola in one word. The responses speak for themselves: essential, invaluable, indispensable, unifying and entertaining.

9 LESSONS ABOUT COMMUNITY ENGAGEMENT

40. Be a force for good in the community

Human beings are, at heart, highly social beings and crave to belong. We want to be connected to one another in an increasingly technology-led world. This urge became even stronger during the pandemic, when people around the globe had to get used to the idea of staying at home and self-isolating. It hasn't helped our growing sense of isolation that major institutions, from political parties and churches to NATO and the EU, seem to be weakening. Fears of the unknown have forced many people to retreat a little further, finding cohesion on a smaller scale by valuing their communities even more. We've found comfort by making a difference in a small way at a local level. The power of community, whether on a geographic basis or as a set of individuals with a common ideal, is now significant, with 94 per cent of us agreeing that it feeds our emotions with entertainment, inspiration and joy (Capper 2021). Meanwhile, schools and clubs are experiencing squeezed budgets. Even previously wealthy schools have had to offer reduced choices for pupils and many clubs and societies are wholly dependent on volunteers and local fundraising efforts.

With millions of transactions recorded each day, retailers have endless opportunities to interact face to face with the public and make a difference. Physical stores in particular provide the perfect hub for people to engage with one another and work together to overcome key social, economic and environmental challenges. National retailers with hundreds or thousands of stores have hundreds or thousands of opportunities to demonstrate that, as well as being a major chain, they can also be a hub for local communities. Their presence gives them a natural advantage over online retailers.

There are ample examples of how retailers have been a force for good in local communities, nudging like-minded groups to work together for the good of the area they live and work in. Stores can use their physical position to encourage formal or informal community networks to combine forces and work together towards a common goal. During the pandemic, retailers became adept at using their sheer size and reach to do everything from becoming makeshift vaccine and testing centres to acting as collection and distribution points for food banks. Post pandemic, we've seen a return to store-based community activities such as fundraising bake sales or raffle draws being held at store entrances.

Reward programmes offer retailers a golden opportunity to formalise and expand upon their role at the heart of communities.

Reward programmes offer retailers a golden opportunity to formalise and expand upon their role at the heart of communities. This will, in return, create a positive perception of those retailers. Individual shoppers will forget that their local grocery store is part of a significant national or international chain. What matters to shoppers is that frequenting their local store opens up an opportunity to help schools or sports clubs in the immediate area. It's irrelevant to them that the chain may be doing exactly the same thing in thousands of other locations.

Aldi is a great example of a major chain that has been successfully pursuing this strategy for some time. In each location where they open up, anywhere in the world, they adapt their promotions to the local market, supporting homegrown interests in everything from Australian football to Farm Africa. Even though Aldi is a German discounter, these initiatives mean that customers in each region view the retailer as proudly 'Australian' or 'African' or whatever other market it opens in. It makes absolute commercial sense to fly the local flag.

A community campaign could be as simple as offering Apple computers to students, which stores such as Coles in Australia started doing more than 30 years ago, as did the Giant supermarket chain on the east coast of the United States. As time has gone by, this has progressed to a mechanic where shoppers have the option to donate any points collected from a general programme to local organisations trying to raise funds. Rather than redeeming points for their own benefit, customers can also opt to help their communities. We've been designing programmes with this mechanic for some years. This itself has also developed, moving towards dual rewards options, where points can be collected towards rewards for both the individual and good causes.

There are of course, many more strategies that build a strong bespoke community campaign. A good starting point is to understand how shoppers benefit from belonging to a community. In general, the answer lies in two key areas: a sense of personal fulfilment together with a feeling of being part of something. As Figure 10 illustrates, shoppers enjoy the fact that when they take part in activities to help their communities they feel seen and appreciated for their efforts. They get a good vibe from embracing the lifestyle choice of caring for others. Meanwhile, by becoming more involved in their community, they cultivate a sense of 'we' and being accepted by others. Joining forces with others creates the potential to achieve something effective.

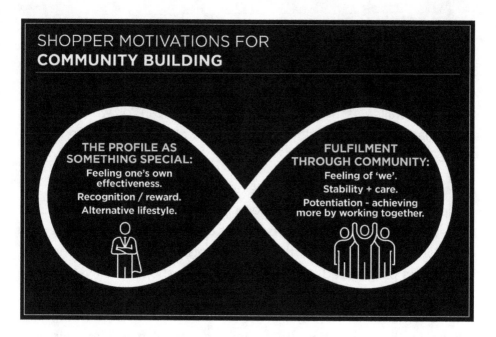

Figure 10 (Source: TCC)

The opportunity here is for retailers to multiply the positive impact their customers feel by playing a role in their communities. When customers are able to do something active towards helping local good causes it helps them build on that feeling of personal responsibility. By encouraging shoppers to actively do something, ie collect points, retailers are opening up opportunities for them to achieve recognition. At the same time, such a campaign can reinforce a shopper's sense of fulfilment through helping the community by giving them easy and uncomplicated tasks. Shoppers want to do something worthwhile but they want control over how much or how little of their time they devote to this activity. Nothing could be simpler than collecting a few points at the till but it can make a huge difference to cash-strapped clubs, societies and schools.

A big advantage of any community campaign is that it gets people talking. In fact, the opportunity can be viewed as a social network in itself. In the past, information exchange between loyalty programme collectors, either directly or online, was perceived to be a 'soft benefit' of campaigns. Today, it should be looked upon as a significant driver in unifying communities both real and virtual and helping to keep everyone in touch. Not only does it create a conversation at the point of sale, but discussion of the event will also filter out into the neighbourhood. Adults and children at clubs will swap notes on the promotion and encourage others to get involved. Programmes should be adapted to include greater opportunities for customer to customer interaction, gamification and points swaps, encouraging collectors to feel more connected with one another as well as the retailer that facilitates the platform.

A big advantage of any community campaign is that it gets people talking. In fact, the opportunity can be viewed as a social network in itself.

41. Design rewards around community needs

Experience shows that, to be successful, community campaigns have a specific set of requirements. Campaigns must:

▶ be created by retailers with a significant national presence. To have maximum impact there needs to be a sign-up of a large percentage of schools/sports centres because shoppers expect their local supermarket to be supporting causes in their immediate area.

▶ offer rewards that are 100 per cent free. Asking shoppers to collect points for, say, computers for schools but then expecting an additional €50 to secure each one will not connect. It has to be seen as a gift.

▶ be highly visible in-store. This is crucial for arousing curiosity and participation.

▶ drive the message home that 'together we are strong' through repeated use of language such as 'we' instead of 'I'. In other words, the real donors are shoppers, not the retailer, since shoppers are giving their vouchers to their preferred clubs. This increases emotional participation.

▶ make sure no one feels excluded. Participation should be encouraged from small clubs, private and public schools and those offering less popular sports and activities.

▶ provide a wide range of opportunities to participate, from dedicated websites to physical options such as putting a box at the end of cash desks, so shoppers can insert points there and then.

▶ always provide up-to-date information, indicating points redemption and celebrating rewards and objectives reached.

▶ keep the focus on the community performance, not the retailer's achievements.

▶ personalise the campaign by highlighting wins at participating schools or clubs or publishing profiles of sports coaches. Every opportunity should be taken for public interaction with partner clubs.

Making an impact in a community campaign might appear like no small undertaking but the benefits can and do significantly outweigh the effort required. Many institutions such as schools and clubs have suffered from years of underfunding and the problems that need to be addressed can be substantial. Communities will respond positively to these campaigns and also look kindly on the retailers that provide the rewards. Big ticket items such as a school computer or substantial piece of sports equipment will remain a constant visual reminder of the store that enabled it, long after the promotion ends.

If the goal is particularly ambitious, it may make sense to bring in a partner. We have, for example, worked with the WWF, the European Space Agency, Disney and UNICEF. Their contribution was different in each case but each time these international organisations added huge value, whether it was contributing resources, supplying experts to speak at schools or clubs or vetting promotional material. The sum of the parts really is greater than the whole since partnerships offer the potential to reach a wider customer base. There's no compulsion to partner with just one organisation. Multiple participating brands offer even more opportunities for customers to be inspired at a range of different touchpoints. Individuals can earn points when they visit retailers but the partners are the bait that draws them to the particular stores in the first place.

Big ticket items such as a school computer or substantial piece of sports equipment will remain a constant visual reminder of the store that enabled it, long after the promotion ends.

42. Make community campaigns fun

As previously stated, creating a buzz and excitement around a rewards programme is crucial to its success, which is why so much effort needs to be put into launching it and then maintaining the momentum with a succession of in-store events. What's particularly powerful about a community rewards campaign is that the most impactful in-store events are often not in-store at all. The events are in local schools or sports clubs or whatever the focus is of the campaign. The beneficiaries of the schemes will take on the task of drumming up interest because the more their friends, colleagues and fellow parents get involved, the better off the whole community will be. (This is not to say that the key role of individual store managers is diminished in any way – they're still at the centre of all efforts to excite shoppers and ensure complete buy-in.)

How far a retailer can go to encourage this will vary country by country. In Italy, for example, schools are content to display large rewards prominently on site. If the promotion requires x number of points to acquire, say, a new computer, a computer can be displayed prominently in the reception area. Don't forget to pick up your points! Collect them now. Other countries have strict rules that forbid such overt advertising onsite. In France, branded material is not permitted on school premises, which is in part why community campaigns there are not as common. If promotional material is not allowed, stores will need to shoulder the bulk of the task of creating a buzz. However, once the community becomes involved, campaigns always gain momentum outside the store. Collectors will canvas families and friends to collect and may even organise informal events themselves.

Most importantly, community campaigns should be fun. They become a focal point for people with a common interest to rally around. Since the campaign will only run for a limited time, there is an incentive for everyone in the community to throw themselves into it and create events to help everyone feel involved. What better way to inspire and engage people than doing something that will put a smile on their faces and the faces of those they help?

43. Design rewards around healthy eating and wellness

Healthy living is a concern for more than half of the world's population (54 per cent) and obesity continues to be a major concern. Worldwide, more than 1.9 billion adults and 39 million children are overweight or obese, a threefold rise since 1975 (WHO 2021). Much of this is down to changing eating habits, in particular increased consumption of processed foods such as chocolate, chips and snacks. Widespread information campaigns mean many people are already translating their concerns into action with 43 per cent actively checking the labels/nutritional information on the products they buy and more than a third reducing their consumption of packaged food (37 per cent) and sweets (38 per cent) (Win International 2020).

One of the consequences of a period of high inflation and rising prices in stores is many families won't eat as well. The priority will be lower-priced food rather than buying food with a high nutritional value. Retailers have long been viewed as an important partner when it comes to taking responsibility for how we shop and cook and have responded well by playing an active role in reinforcing nutrition education strategies. In fact, there's no major chain anywhere in the world that doesn't have 'helping customers live healthier lives' as part of their strategy. The impact that retailers can have on consumer health and lifestyle choices can be seen in a range of different ways. In many regions, retailers have reacted to pressure by removing sugary treats from areas around tills to reduce last-minute temptation for impulse buys and relieve parents from pester power.

Elsewhere, retailers have taken an active role in moving away from stocking unhealthy products. In 2015, for example, the US retail pharmacy company CVS Health took cigarettes off its shelves for good, leading to a $2 billion drop in annual sales via tobacco. The chain, which made up turnover via other initiatives, won plaudits from public health officials thanks to the 1 per cent reduction in cigarette sales (95 million packs) across 13 states in the first eight months of taking them off the shelves. Of those customers who quit the habit, just 38 per cent were CVS Health regulars. The rest of the drop in sales came from other retailers.

Loyalty campaigns also play a vital role in promoting the retailer's role as a consumer's wellness partner.

Loyalty campaigns also play a vital role in promoting the retailer's role as a consumer's wellness partner. Rewards can be designed around healthy eating and wellness, with collections that support endeavours such as home cooking, increased use of fresh food and better education about nutrition. Rewards can play a key role here in a variety of ways.

▶ The choice of the rewards themselves pushes the message that home cooking doesn't need to be difficult and time consuming. When you have a beautiful range of chef-worthy cooking utensils, knives and cooking aids, spending time in the kitchen seems more attractive. Well-chosen rewards can ease a shopper's life and help elevate their cooking skills to the next level. Once they get into the habit, it will inspire them to move away from heavily processed products.

▶ The points-collecting mechanic can also be a crucial part of the 'eat fresh' message. Additional points can be earned for buying specific goods such as fruit and vegetables and other home cooking staples. When shoppers are rewarded for making healthy choices it encourages them to be more adventurous.

▶ There are also opportunities to extend campaigns with omnichannel solutions such as online recipes and competitions focused on fresh food. Dedicated apps can help families to manage their fridges and freezers so they know how long food has been there and nothing will go to waste.

▶ Rewards can be designed around specific health messages. In the past, we've run campaigns giving away fitness bikes in Hong Kong, Beurer blood pressure and heart monitors in Switzerland and air purifiers in Germany.

44. Design rewards around children's education and nutrition

As every parent knows, it's challenging to get children to eat fresh fruit and vegetables. The solution: make it playful. We've seen a lot of success with this simple yet effective mechanic. Biedronka, Poland's leading hypermarket chain, used this strategy to encourage children to be more adventurous at mealtimes. The Goodness Gang, a colourful collection of plush fruit and vegetable toy rewards (first mentioned in lesson 13), became highly collectable. Children may not have realised it but the Goodness Gang encouraged a subtle shift in their minds. The sense of suspicion and mistrust that many youngsters experienced around fruit and veg was replaced by a sense of fun and joy around the characters. Parents were aware of the shift in outlook. Biedronka received multiple communications along the lines of 'My son never took to his greens but this campaign really helped him try'.

Omnichannel campaigns offer the opportunity to reinforce and build upon the healthy eating message. Gamification, for example, can engage children, providing another touchpoint to find out more about characters such as the Goodness Gang and get involved in their adventures. At each of these touchpoints, messages can be added, which all contribute towards creating long-term behaviour change.

LOYALTY LEGENDS

Get Active – Scheine für vereine/vouchers for sports clubs: Rewe, Germany

Sports clubs and leisure centres play an essential role in our physical wellbeing and provide a crucial social outlet too. Many clubs worldwide face chronic underfunding, with their situation becoming even more perilous during the Covid-19 lockdowns. In many cases, retailers such as Rewe in Germany stepped in to take up the slack, taking on a much-needed role as a wellness partner for its customers and local communities.

Rewe, which is Germany's second largest supermarket chain with a market share of 11 per cent across 4,000 stores, already has strong links to sport. It sponsors the national football team as well as the women's team in its home town of Cologne. In autumn 2019, it turned its attention to the 90,000 local sports clubs in Germany, ranging from running tracks to tennis clubs. Germany is one of the most active nations in Europe but was there a way they could help more local communities to stay active and healthy? The answer was yes, and the 'Scheine für vereine' (vouchers for sports clubs) promotion was launched.

The pre-campaign stage of the promotion involved sending out kits to clubs to encourage them to get involved. Their participation was key since club officials and coaches would be central players in whipping up enthusiasm for the promotion. If they got this right their club members, particularly children, would get active, canvassing family, friends and neighbours to collect. They might even patrol cash registers to gather up additional points. Each club was asked to define which reward they'd like their members and local communities to save for. The rewards they could choose from ranged in price scale from the modest, such as team T-shirts and hoodies, to the ambitious, such as a new playground.

Once the campaign launched, every euro spent in a Rewe supermarket or online rewarded customers with vouchers, which included a QR or alphanumerical code. Customers were able to allocate points earned to their chosen local clubs by entering the code into a dedicated website. Each participating club was allocated a page on the website, displaying details about the equipment they were saving for, the number of points required and how many points had been redeemed to date.

To build up excitement, the vouchers mimicked the size and shape of Monopoly money. The mechanic subtly reinforced the idea of communities working and playing together and having time for one another. The playful theme continued through the flyers used to promote the campaign, which featured images of tennis balls being tipped over a young woman's head, in a similar vein to the popular ice bucket challenge. The slogan for the campaign was simple and to the point: make your sports club happy.

Rewe's role in the campaign was very much as an enabler. They were the link between shoppers and local clubs, creating the environment where it all happened. While Rewe is a large, national brand, the intention was to bring the focus down to a single store, harnessing the power and passion of collective social responsibility. In return, Rewe was able to strengthen its own position in the local community.

A clear sign that the community had taken the campaign to heart was when shoppers began to influence subtle changes in the promotion. For example, shortly after the campaign launched, it was noted that some cashiers had used their own initiative and placed shoe boxes at the end of their tills to collect vouchers. This was, it transpired, in response to requests from less digitally savvy customers who found handing over vouchers easier than logging on to allocate their points. After that, Rewe produced bespoke boxes that were left on the end of tills so that shoppers had the option of dropping off their tickets straight away.

In another example of communities owning the campaign, Rewe's initial TV promotion featuring Bayern Munich football star Thomas Müller received muted feedback. It emerged that communities preferred 'keeping it real'. Later TV commercials switched to use footage from real clubs and participants were also invited to submit their own footage. Rewe's Christmas TV commercials featured videos of members of amateur sportsmen and women voicing their thanks to shoppers for helping them and their clubs so much through the promotion.

The 2019 Scheine für vereine promotion distributed equipment to 55,000 clubs, with a combined value of more than €13 million. Since then, Rewe has run this campaign twice more, in 2020 and 2022. The 2020 campaign was particularly poignant since so many people were in lockdown and unable to visit their local clubs. In this case, social media was an invaluable part of the campaign. More than 23,000 social media posts and 7,000 promotional videos maintained the community mood as everyone sought to support their clubs and keep them in play for when everyone returned for better times.

LOYALTY LEGENDS

The magnetic power of private label: Coop Italia

As all grocery retailers know, own label is an important part of the mix, not least because the margins are often far higher than on branded goods. There are, however, other reasons to increase the share of own label. Boosting sales of own label helps retailers become less reliant on industry suppliers and to differentiate their offer from competitors. In recent years, retailers have also been waking up to the idea that own label has another important part to play in the mix: the ideal opportunity to project their values. This was thinking behind a campaign by Coop Italia after an exercise to revamp 2,000 of its own label products.

Coop Italia's reformulated and relabelled own label products became the star of the show in the Frighissimi rewards programme. Twenty-four of the retailer's own label items were recreated in miniature as fridge magnets, with three of them as highly collectable glow-in-the-dark items. For every €10 spent in-store, customers would receive a sachet containing one magnet. The promotion caught on quickly, which was in great part helped by a range of supporting material. Customers could, for example, spend €1.99 to buy one or two versions of a 'completer' board on which to store their miniature magnets if they didn't fancy keeping them on their fridge. Also on sale was a dedicated board game, centring around the 24 products, with the dual aim of helping to communicate the value of own label in endeavours such as recycling and healthy eating. Those that preferred the digital medium were not forgotten either. Unique codes on the flow packs could be used to log into a website to play an own label themed game, as well as receive vouchers. The 'jackpot' prize was a relatively modest €27,000, yet more than 2.5 million customers logged on to try their luck. As well as activities for kids, the bespoke website also boasted plenty of creative ideas and videos on how to recycle and reuse packaging. During the six weeks of the promotion, there were more than one million sessions online and seven million page views, elevating the Frighissimi website into the top 100 in Italy.

The entire Frighissimi campaign was supported in-store with extensive signage and displays, mascot events, offering photo opportunities with life-size versions of the magnets, and playground areas where kids could play a maxi version of the promotion's board game.

The mark of success of any campaign is when it takes on a life of its own. During the six-week period during which it ran, the Frighissimi characters became viral stars online as customers posted their pictures of their collections. One Instagram user even shared a shot of their car covered with dozens of the magnets. 'Collect them all,' posted a Facebook user, with a picture of the magnets proudly spread across their kitchen table. Informal swap groups proliferated and a lively market emerged on eBay, with the magnets changing hands at €20 each. Overall, 13 million magnets were collected. The campaign met its goal, boosting own label sales 10.5 per cent year on year, and a 151 per cent ROI.

10 LESSONS ABOUT THE FUTURE OF LOYALTY

45. Ride the third wave

Since the inception of The Continuity Company three decades ago, we have worked through three distinct waves of retail activity. When we started out, the retail business was entirely product driven. The focus of this first wave was on offering a great assortment of products to attract customers and encourage them to fill their trolleys. Merchandise solutions were flagged in-store with large-scale displays. During the second wave, we saw a switch to a more retail-centric approach. Retailers began to place greater emphasis on low price offers, selecting the right mix of products to stock on their shelves and boosting sales with promotions. This was a period when we saw a significant shift towards embracing rewards programmes. Store groups came to understand that a loyalty campaign could lift sales by between 3 and 5 per cent compared to cut-price offers, which might boost sales by 0.5 per cent or, if the retailer was really lucky, by up to 1 per cent. This was a breakthrough period for loyalty as we saw campaign after campaign genuinely change customer behaviour in the long term.

We've now entered the third wave, which is truly consumer driven. In reality, we've been heading in this direction for some time but, like so many things, the pandemic significantly accelerated the trend, possibly by up to a decade. Then, to add to this, at the time of writing we're entering a tough economic period. Meanwhile, there are so many options on offer to customers today, including retailers that offer goods at a significant discount. All retailers have to offer customers a positive experience every time or will miss out to competitors that do offer customers what they want.

46. Keep up with retail trends

Here are the seven most significant trends we've identified in the third wave.

1. Online

Over the course of the pandemic, 75 per cent of consumers adopted new shopping behaviours prompted by a range of factors, from store closures to economic pressure and changed personal circumstances (Charm et al 2020). In the first year of the pandemic, ecommerce's share of all retail sales globally grew from 16 to 19 per cent. There are significant regional variations, though. In South Korea, internet sales grew from one in five transactions to one in four, while in the US the range was 11 per cent rising to 14 per cent (United Nations 2021). In all cases, though, the indications are: digital shopping is definitely here to stay. The growth in customers purchasing online is forecast to be in the range of between 15 and 30 per cent across all categories from groceries to fashion, medicine and personal care (Briedis et al 2020).

What is it that customers like so much about shopping online? Why are they so likely to stick with the new habit? Ease and convenience always score highly in surveys, as do low prices. It's far easier to shop around using a search engine, plus there's the opportunity to join rewards programmes and have deals sent straight to our inboxes.

2. Zero friction delivery

Even before the pandemic we were seeing changes in how customers shopped and received their goods. The shift was, at least in part, prompted by dissatisfaction with visits to retail locations. Shoppers cited that long running bugbear, frustration with queues at the checkout, as well as irritation about navigating crowded aisles or being unable to quickly locate the required item. For some people, though, a complete switch to online wasn't an option. Online does, after all, present challenges too, not least to those who aren't in a position to stay at home all day to wait for a delivery. As a result, a hybrid online to offline model had already gained in popularity before the pandemic. In the US, retailers such as Walmart and Target have built a significant business in curbside pick-ups, while in France the drive-through model has become a favoured option for fulfilling orders. Social distancing rules accelerated the trend and there has been a significant year on year increase (28 per cent) in 'buy online, pick up in-store' (BOPIS), also known as click and collect (Briedis et al 2020). BOPIS, curbside and drive-through are forecast to continue to grow for a range of reasons. One in particular is that these options offer a solution to the problem of delayed gratification, which has long been seen as a drawback to ecommerce. Once a customer clicks 'buy', they often have to wait at least 24 hours for their order to arrive. (Although some retailers do offer same-day delivery.) Click and collect orders can be fulfilled and ready for pick up in less than an hour. There's also the prospect of more convenient returns. Rather than having to initiate a return via mail or courier, if a product is not right, BOPIS customers can view items on pick-up and even return in the same visit if needed.

3. Ordering in

There was a time when the only competition supermarkets needed to consider was their near rivals. Today's major competitors hail from all directions. There are food delivery apps, which bring complete meals direct to our doorsteps. Platform to consumer services such as Deliveroo, DoorDash and Uber Eats deliver every type of food you can imagine. The online services make full use of route optimisation technology for their extensive network of drivers, which guarantees faster and cheaper delivery. For those households that enjoy home cooking, there are a growing number of meal kit firms that deliver boxes full of raw ingredients. The beauty of these services, run by businesses such as Germany-based Hello Fresh, is that consumers can enjoy the creativity of cooking and perhaps even a bit of experimentation. The added advantage is that there's less food waste, since portion sizes are carefully measured. UK food charity WRAP reports a 34 per cent reduction in wasted potatoes, bread, milk and chicken, as households manage their food more efficiently using meal kits. The global value of the food delivery market is forecast to reach $140 billion in 2022 but within five years is expected to soar to $300 billion (Curry 2023). Much of this will be market share taken from supermarkets.

4. Income disparities

Global inflation is at its highest level since the financial crisis of 2008. There are a number of reasons for this trend, from rising demand for energy and petrol and shortages of goods following pandemic factory shutdowns to rising supply chain and shipping costs and wage increases as employers struggle to fill jobs. The war in Ukraine has exacerbated what was already a pressing issue and is likely to do so for some time to come. Campaigners have warned that the crisis will disproportionately impact those already in poverty. With rises in rent, petrol and taxes, many households will have to significantly cut back on food and other household expenditure. It's inevitable that fast-growing discounters such as Aldi and Lidl will benefit as families significantly cut back on their food shopping and try to save wherever possible.

5. Consolidation of shopper behaviour

Because of recent lockdowns and their associated trading restrictions, shoppers in the UK for example are now less likely to find everything they need on the high street, with 9,300 fewer retail outlets open in March 2022 compared to March 2020 (Easton 2022). However, the big supermarket chains were operating 194 more stores in the UK by the end of Covid-19 restrictions, up 2.5 per cent. There's an increasing focus on value, especially regarding essentials. It's also more convenient to use home delivery for heavy or bulk-buy commodities, from loo roll to tinned food. Visits to shops are increasingly reserved for items we prefer to see and feel, such as fresh food.

There are already ample signs that supermarkets are on top of making changes to accommodate this trend. We've moved on from the position where, even just a few years ago, stores around the world were competing for larger and larger real estate. Chains would build stores spanning more than 9,000 square metres, with banks of checkouts to serve customers. Today, many big retailers are cutting down on that real estate and moving to a more local store model. In the physical locations that remain, there has been a reimagining of the store network to focus on customer experience, so when customers do venture out, they enjoy their visit.

6. Health priorities

One of the inevitable trends that developed during the pandemic was that shoppers wanted to spend less time in stores. An increased sense of empathy for others and a desire to protect ourselves meant we'd go in, get what we needed and leave. There was no time to hang around, browse and be inspired by offers. This is a trend that has yet to go away and many retailers are adapting to the prospect that future interactions with customers will be defined by health and safety expectations. With speed and convenience being key, the foundation of customer service – face-to-face interaction – is being replaced by virtual or contactless touchpoints.

7. Reprioritisation of values

The full stop to our lives prompted by successive lockdowns gave many of us pause to reconsider our life choices and, in many cases, led to a reprioritisation of values. For many, the focus settled upon maintaining optimum health and fitness. The food we eat is an important part of maintaining a healthy lifestyle and there has been a noticeable rise in interest in fresh and healthy foods. The global health and wellness food market, which was valued at $733.1 billion in 2020, is forecast to increase to $1 trillion by 2026 (Shahbandeh 2022). In addition, as detailed previously, there has been a significant growth in interest in sustainability, regeneration and community issues.

47. Rise to the digital challenge

The third wave presents challenges to retailers on multiple fronts but there's one unifying factor at the centre of much of it: digital. While online sales are still in the minority, at between 10 and 20 per cent, this is increasingly being viewed as the area where loyalty will be built and retailers will differentiate from one another. Traditionally, the shift to online has been particularly tough on those retailers with an established physical store portfolio, since many found it difficult to make money out of home delivery. Creating/strengthening a credible digital infrastructure does not come cheap and it's almost impossible to pass on the full costs to the customer. This is particularly so when it comes to the cost of transporting goods to customers' homes. One of the aspects of online that shoppers say they value most is free delivery. More than half of online customers (50.2 per cent) cite this as their main motivation (Oberlo 2022) for choosing one store over another. It represents a great deal for shoppers to have their goods packed and delivered at no cost, rather than visiting a store to physically view and inspect products before paying at the till, but at the same time it's tough for a retailer's bottom line. Likewise, while BOPIS is handy for customers, offering a quick and easy pick-up process, it can be labour intensive and time consuming for retailers. It can be particularly tricky during busy periods or when there is a sudden increase in orders, which puts pressure on the teams charged with fulfilling the order.

While online sales are still in the minority, at between 10 and 20 per cent, this is increasingly being viewed as the area where loyalty will be built and retailers will differentiate from one another.

Retailers are now beginning to resolve these issues. While the cost to pick and deliver product ordered online is still a loss leader, it's becoming less and less so as more innovative solutions are found. The losses can also be balanced out by basket size. On average, people tend to buy twice as much product online versus a trip to a physical store, therefore the margin gains from these online shopping baskets are higher.

However, product margins or delivery charges won't determine the success of retail online operations in the future. The key to growing online profitability lies in relevance. Retailers need to be relevant to every single customer on an individual basis and offer the solutions that these customers are looking for. One of the big values of online is, after all, that customer behaviour can be tracked. Retailers are able to scrutinise the shopping patterns of individuals and predict future patterns. Our buying patterns tell retailers if we're single, have children, or if our eating habits are changing to become more health conscious. Once retailers are armed with this knowledge, they're better able to reflect their customers' needs and wants in order to build market share. Online retailers can already pre-select a customer's weekly shopping list, based on their previous purchases. They may not get every product right but if it's at least 70 per cent correct it's a huge time saver for the customer. The next logical step is for retailers to use these insights to influence customer choices in the future, using data to deepen online strategy.

The key to growing online profitability lies in relevance. Retailers need to be relevant to every single customer on an individual basis and offer the solutions that these customers are looking for.

The next stage is for retailers to follow the lead of established online-only businesses such as Amazon and monetise their core expertise. Amazon doesn't focus on making profit on the products it sells. Most of its operating profits are boosted by other sources such as its Amazon Prime membership. Among other things, Prime offers entertainment content. While this presents a high fixed cost to Amazon for buying rights or producing shows, it enhances the appeal of being a Prime member. Prime membership, in turn, encourages people to switch more and more of their online and offline spending to Amazon. Elsewhere, Amazon opens its platform to huge numbers of third party businesses to sell their products through Amazon's own platform. The fees charged to these vendors represent 25 per cent of Amazon's revenue (Cuofano 2023).

Retailers have a massive reach and there are few other organisations in the world that know more about customers than food retailers, particularly now, thanks to digital. That knowledge is extremely relevant to major brands and something they're more than prepared to invest in. Imagine, for example, a brand such as Unilever is launching a sustainable range and wants to build brand awareness among its target customers. It could go down the traditional route, investing extensively in TV and press advertising together with an online campaign, or it could work with retailers to 'speak' directly to shoppers that have already shown a predisposition towards sustainability as illustrated by their online browsing history. It's early days but retailers are already seizing the opportunity and working closely with big third party brands to target individual customers with offers that are highly specific to their interests.

Retailers are already seizing the opportunity and working closely with big third party brands to target individual customers with offers that are highly specific to their interests.

While we can, in the future, expect to see retailers encouraging more and more customers to move online, this cannot be the only focus. The future is definitely omnichannel. Shoppers still want to do at least some of their shopping in person, which means physical stores remain an important part of the mix. The focus here, now more than ever, is to create an unforgettable in-store experience. Plus, as detailed previously, physical stores also take up an important position at the centre of communities, which is another strong driver of customer behaviour today. We certainly expect to see many more community focused campaigns.

48. Learn from the latest research

As outlined previously, we use an extensive range of research on shopper behaviour, both internal and external. It plays a vital part in designing programmes that fulfil the needs of retailers and their customers and enables us to continue evolving and creating successful loyalty strategies. One particular piece of research was released just as I was finishing writing this book and I was heartened to find that it supports most of our recommendations. Despite being UK-centric, it has relevance to many other territories in which we operate.

This white paper, created by loyalty specialist Mando-Connect in partnership with research data and analytics group YouGov (conducted in January 2022), sets out to examine what Brits want from loyalty programmes. The overarching finding was that the UK is still a nation of loyalty lovers, with 70 per cent of shoppers currently being members of a loyalty programme. An equal percentage believe that these programmes are a great way for brands and businesses to reward customers.

The number one driver for British consumers to join a loyalty programme is the rewards. Sixty per cent join for discounts and offers, 28 per cent for partner rewards and 23 per cent for free products, services, experiences and privileges. Rewards are also the top driver of engagement, with 52 per cent saying that good offers, rewards and benefits that are constantly changing and updating keep them loving and using programmes.

The number one driver for British consumers to join a loyalty programme is the rewards.

The results of the research also underlined the importance of sustainability and helping the environment. Seventy-one per cent of Brits think loyalty programmes should help people live more sustainably or support the environment while 44 per cent want programmes to reward sustainable/environmentally friendly behaviours. They want rewards that help them live more sustainably too (43 per cent) and, of course, they want programmes to support environmental charities like so many already do (39 per cent). This all goes to prove, yet again, that a strong sustainability ethos needs to be baked into loyalty programmes.

So, do Brits love loyalty more than any other nation in the world? That wasn't part of the research but it's clear that not even the pandemic has dented their faith in the positive impact of loyalty programmes – on customers' hearts, heads and wallets.

49. Be a force for good in the world

One of the best decisions we made at TCC was back in 2017, when we started a foundation with a vision to create brighter beginnings for some of the world's most disadvantaged children in meaningful and innovative ways. We focused on three pillars: healthy eating and nutrition, protecting vulnerable children and tackling child hunger. To bring this alive, we started donating 5 per cent of our annual profits and matching our colleagues' fundraising initiatives across all of our 34 offices.

In our own small way we've been able to support more than 100 projects around the world donating close to €5 million to these good causes with such great organisations as Save the Children, Amnesty International, Medicines sans Frontières, Action Aid and many others.

Not only have we done some good in the world but we've also seen how doing good can bind our teams together in special ways and in a great spirit.

Our employee giving programme and online platform, TCC Gives, was launched a year ago and already €398,000 has been donated to almost 100 good causes that our colleagues care most about. Within TCC Gives, the team has been having their say in where funds and support go, through the new TCC Foundation long service award scheme, matched donations and TCC's introduction of paid volunteering days. The programme has been empowering colleagues to get involved and make a difference.

We are, of course, in the loyalty business and I truly believe that by being a force for good the TCC Foundation has helped us to attract and retain the best people in our industry.

50. Loyalty is still the answer

The big question is: what benefits will loyalty bring in the future? Is our business model still relevant? The answer is a resounding yes. In fact, we believe that rewards are more important than ever, particularly right now. With rising inflation and household budgets tighter than ever before, the idea of a shop rewarding loyalty by giving customers something for nothing has never been more appropriate. For families labouring under the burden of ever-rising prices, it may feel as if every business is trying to get something more from them. A retailer that gives something away for free as a thank you for shopping with them will earn the trust, respect and enduring gratitude of their customers.

For retailers themselves, loyalty programmes still represent the most powerful, cost-effective way to reward customers because they minimise wasted marketing spend. They are more effective than conventional discount-led promotions, which are indiscriminate, offering money off to everyone, regardless of whether or not they are a regular shopper. As outlined earlier, a loyalty campaign provides for a 5–8 per cent reward on shopper spend. A money off discount offer is equivalent to a 1 per cent reward on spend.

It's questionable to put 1 or 2 per cent of the cost price of goods into discount promotions, instead of investing a quarter of one per cent in a loyalty campaign. Plus, a well-structured loyalty campaign typically drives a 3 to 4 per cent lift in total store sales over a 16-week period. Loyalty promotions also secure far better engagement from shoppers and genuinely differentiate any retailer from its competitors.

Let's not forget either that the pendulum has swung firmly towards relationships with customers, who want to be treated as individuals. The foundation of loyalty has always centred around establishing a deep and lasting bond between customer and retailer. Retailers can still spend money on discounts to keep up that all important cost-conscious perception but with just a small shift of promotional funds retailers can genuinely have the best of both worlds by building an emotional connection too.

The foundation of loyalty has always centred around establishing a deep and lasting bond between customer and retailer.

While the fundamentals of loyalty will remain the same, there will need to be some changes to meet the challenges of the third wave. The impact retailers want to have has changed and so must the loyalty programmes they run. That's why our business also needs to change to reflect that.

In the third wave, the focus of loyalty will be on building the right experience, for the right audience. We believe loyalty will come into its own in the following ways:

Omnichannel loyalty: The bulk of all future campaigns will be omnichannel and geared towards rewarding specific behaviour where people shop. There will be much more innovation in reward mechanics across various platforms as retailers increasingly drive customers towards spending in particular categories or to reward them for lifestyle choices such as health and wellbeing. Facilitating online platforms where customers can reach out to one another will also be key, to build awareness and support promotions. TCC is growing its own digital capabilities via a new sister business, Drivvn, which has already become what we believe is one of the biggest online sellers of vehicles in Europe (AM Online 2023). They are focused on a true omnichannel approach, joining together national sales companies and retailers to ensure everyone has the same view of each customer and increasing conversion to sale. There have been several ecommerce milestones, with the Citroen AMI sold purely online in all markets, while customers are increasingly comfortable making large purchases and some brands now have more than 20 per cent of all purchases being made online.

Facilitating online platforms where customers can reach out to one another will also be key, to build awareness and support promotions.

Personalisation: This is about reaching individual customers and being relevant to them and we'll undoubtedly see more personalisation in loyalty campaigns. In fact, we're already seeing this happening in a limited sense. If customers spend online, they might receive the first set of points for free to encourage future collection. This already creates a difference between those who spend online and those who don't. Then, moving on, as stores improve their understanding of customer behaviour, they can reward points according to an individual's preferences. We already know that shoppers need to be incentivised to try something new multiple times in order to break existing patterns. It's only once they have built up some good experiences that they're willing to change. Thus if, say, a shopper prefers gluten-free food, they can be offered points for every gluten-free purchase. Over time, this highly targeted promotion discourages shoppers from going elsewhere, creating a firm bond and setting in train that regular pattern of behaviour. A retailer that wants to see more shoppers buying fresh on a Monday can change its points system to reward those most likely to buy fresh but who usually shop at the weekend. The key to success in personalised offers is customer awareness and in greater understanding of how customers want to be contacted. Retailers need to talk to customers via the channels they prefer. Some live on social media, for example, rather than constantly checking through emails. Therefore push-through offers via social make sense.

The key to success in personalised offers is customer awareness and in greater understanding of how customers want to be contacted.

Locally targeted campaigns: These represent a huge opportunity for retailers to cement their position at the heart of the community. Individual branches can reward good causes in their immediate environment and provide a platform for customers to support those closest to them. Likewise, there will more online facilities for customers to allocate their rewards to the causes that they feel matter most. Overall, the priority will be to make shopping a more social experience, offering opportunities for real human connections. While it's handy to segment people into a simple box matrix, none of us are bit-part players in a huge crowd. We are individuals and we want to be part of something. Loyalty campaigns help us to celebrate that.

Changed rewards: The selection of rewards on offer will change in line with customers' expectations. We've already seen a trend towards much less focus on products for products' sake. The emphasis is increasingly on how products match the needs of individual customers. The move towards sustainability has been a big driver of this trend. Even three or four years ago, children were regularly incentivised with rewards of small plastic figurines. That would be completely unthinkable today and, in some regions in particular, could negatively impact the reputation of any organisation that offered them. The once ubiquitous plastic figurine is increasingly being replaced by toys made from recycled plastic or game cards made from biodegradable paper.

There will also be a shift towards non-physical rewards. We've already seen companies such as Nike going into the metaverse with digital rewards. We'll surely see many more non-physical options such as game passes or virtual rewards. TCC has already been looking at non-fungible tokens (NFT), which are completely digital rewards. It's early days but we fully expect to see more of this. Once again, this will be integrated with the core objectives of the retailer offering the promotion.

Gamification: As previously outlined, the gamification of loyalty will continue to grow and expand. We expect to see increasing numbers of digital tie-in campaigns with specific customer goals. To return to sustainability, rewards campaigns could incentivise customers to make sustainable choices and reward them with virtual trees. Once enough points are collected, real trees can be planted in exchange for their virtual counterparts.

Perhaps most importantly of all, customers still love the idea of getting something for free. I'm reminded of a historic interview I once heard with Jeff Bezos. The interviewer was keen to know his views on what was next for Amazon. What changes did he envisage over the next decade? What developments should we be preparing ourselves for? His reply surprised me. Bezos noted that this was a question he was asked all the time. However, it was the wrong question, he said. What was most important to keep an eye on is what won't change. It was unlikely that Amazon customers would demand that the online retailer reduced its range or had slower deliveries, he said. Customers were extremely happy with these aspects of his business. Therefore, this was what Amazon intended to focus upon to keep growing the business. I thought about this in the context of TCC and realised that the one thing that will never change is that shoppers will always enjoy rewards. They will always see through offers that aren't worth it and gravitate towards collecting rewards they truly value.

I'm sure that loyalty programmes will continue to play a largely familiar yet key role in physical stores. Carefully targeted and widely flagged loyalty programmes will go on driving customer engagement, reminding shoppers of the pleasures of in-person shopping. As detailed throughout this book, there are a huge variety of ways to get everyone involved, whether it's via eye-catching point of sale material or the enthusiastic encouragement and participation of staff. Once again, this will all add towards the customer-centric drive towards experiences.

There's no doubt that we're seeing a significant shift in shopping patterns, perhaps the most significant in our 30-plus years of business. Relevance will take up a position at the centre of everything as retailers seek to recognise and reward customers as individuals. From our viewpoint, the more we can do to help retailers to fulfil the new customer-centric challenges, the more successful we will be. Yes, rewards will change, the way points are collected will change and the ways customers will receive rewards will change. Campaigns will feature multiple touchpoints across many channels to open up opportunities to make a mark on every type of shopper journey. However, many of the lessons from the past will still hold true. The strategy of rewarding specific behaviour has always been central to the success of loyalty campaigns. Perhaps most significantly, the joy of receiving something for nothing – just as I did at 16 when I camped in a tent redeemed from Green Shield Stamps – remains a constant. This kind of enduring emotional connection means that loyalty will remain as powerful as ever well into the future.

Winning and retaining loyal shoppers is the best objective any retailer can have. At the heart of shopper loyalty are the wise words, 'Reward the behaviour you seek.' This has always been our core belief.

Winning and retaining loyal shoppers is the best objective any retailer can have.

GLOSSARY

Accrual rate: The rate at which customers earn points in a rewards programme, eg 1 point for every €1 spent.

Aspirational reward: Generally means a reward with a high perceived value, which customers will aspire to and thus be motivated to change behaviour to collect more points.

Attrition rate: The rate of fall-off among regular collectors who don't go on to collect the full amount of points required to complete a collection.

Back end: All processes that relate to point redemption. (See: Front end.)

BOPIS: An acronym for buy online, pick up in-store.

Breakage: The difference between points issued and rewards redeemed. Breakage may occur when customers drop out, lose interest or don't collect sufficient points to earn the next reward. It also applies when, for example, you receive one point for a €10 spend and four for a €45 spend.

Call to action: Instructions in the rewards promotional campaign. This may include how to register with the programme or details of the points collection process. Continuity programmes have a concrete call to action because they have a finish date, whereas loyalty programmes don't because they often carry on indefinitely without an end date.

Cross-sell: Encouraging customers to buy products from other sections of the store, to build up the requisite number of points.

Current behaviours: Statistics indicating what retail customers do now, including frequency of purchase, purchase characteristics and buying trends. (See: Desired behaviours.)

Customer mobility: Moving customers from one spending category into the next, more profitable tier. Similarly, moving occasional users to become more frequent users.

Customer retention: The ability to sell to customers who have already made a purchase. A retailer's retention metric marks the ability to turn new customers into repeat customers. It's a useful metric to track, as it's among the biggest objectives of any retailer.

Customer segmentation: The grouping of customers into demographic segments using factors such as age, spending, location, income, psychographics and purchase profiles.

Customer value: This is calculated on measures that include frequency of purchase, length of time as a customer and the amount that customer spends in a given time period.

Desired behaviours: Statistics representing what a retailer wants its customers to do in the future, such as spend higher amounts more frequently.

Direct marketing: Direct delivery of advertising and promotional activity that creates and exploits a direct relationship between a retailer and their customers as individuals.

Earn: Describes how a customer accrues points.

Effective funding rate: The actual rate at which customers earn points and rewards, calculated by dividing the price paid for a reward by the amount of currency that needs to be spent to earn sufficient points for the reward.

Enrolment: To become an active member of a loyalty programme often requires enrolment, either online, at the point of purchase or via a call centre. Enrolment makes a customer eligible for rewards.

Equity: The number of points earned.

Financial model: Setting out the forecast expectations for the programme, this document projects enrolment numbers, administrative costs, anticipated points accrual and redemption, leading to the objective of the exercise: a calculation of the programme's ROI.

Front end: All processes that relate to point earning and accrual, such as accrual rate. Can also refer to where the cash registers are located in a supermarket.

Fulfilment: The process by which rewards are put into the hands of a customer who has collected the required number of points. Fulfilment may also include warehousing for the rewards collection, customer service, handling and returns.

Gamification: The application of typical elements of game playing such as point scoring and competition with other players to encourage customers to engage more fully with a loyalty programme. Linking a physical or digital game to a promotional vehicle makes it more exciting and boosts participation.

High-value customer: An economic view of a customer measuring how profitable a customer is to a retailer, as opposed to measuring the profitability of product or service lines.

Liability: As points are issued on a promotion, a percentage of their total value is recorded on the balance sheet as a liability. The percentage of points issued and recorded reflects the total points issued, minus estimated breakage. While it may take time for points to be redeemed, the retailer has pledged to make good on the reward in the future.

Lifetime value: Expected future profits, net of costs, on a customer's transactions. The ultimate goal of a retailer and its loyalty programme is retaining a shopper for life.

Licensing: Licensing is the renting or leasing of an intangible asset. Toys, trading cards and figurines based upon licensed characters from movies and cartoons are popular rewards.

Loyalty marketing: A sales or marketing strategy that rewards loyal customers for repeat business.

NPV: Net present value, or the present value of a customer's total cash inflows and outflows at a given discount rate. NPV determines how much a customer's purchases are worth over time and then discounts that value back to the present.

Omnichannel: Customers are rewarded for any purchase they make, from any channel, online or in-store.

Participation: The percentage of revenue represented by the people taking part in the campaign.

Partner: Another company that participates in a loyalty promotion. The partner can perform a variety of roles, either by supplying rewards or as a retail outlet where participants can also accrue points by purchasing goods and services.

Payout rate: If one point is earned per every euro spent and every point is worth 1 cent, then the payout rate is 1 per cent of all purchases.

Perceived funding rate: The perceived rate at which customers earn points and rewards in a loyalty programme, calculated by dividing the retail price of a reward by the amount of currency that had to be spent to earn the reward.

Perceived value: The imagined monetary value of the rewards by the customer.

Points: Units of currency that signify the amount of customer equity earned by participating in a programme.

Point of sale: POS, as it's more commonly known, represents promotional material located at or near checkouts or a device or system to capture transactions at the time of sale.

Positioning: The positioning, or character, of rewards must match that of the retailer offering the promotion. The type of offer contributes to a customer's perception of the retailer involved.

Promotional material: Material that heightens the excitement around a loyalty programme, which might include posters, games, points collection cards and sweepstakes.

Recency: A measurement of when a customer last interacted with the loyalty programme, such as making a purchase, visiting a website or interacting with a customer contact centre.

Recognition: The act of recognising and thanking customers for their patronage via gifts and rewards.

Redemption: The process of exchanging points for a reward.

Relationship marketing: Building relationships with customers to encourage loyalty, more frequent transactions and a longer relationship with the retailer.

Retention: Customers who make repeat transactions are considered to be retained.

Returns: The number of rewards left unclaimed at the end of a loyalty promotion.

Reward: An item that's acquired via the exchange of points, or other programme currency, following a specified number of purchases.

Rewards earning ratio: The time taken by a typical customer to earn a reward, such as ten shopping trips to gain enough points for one reward.

Targeting: Grouping together best customer prospects to fulfil specific corporate objectives.

Tier: Rewards can be grouped into specific tiers. For example, tier one would consist of rewards up to a value of 5,000 points, tier two groups rewards that can be redeemed for 10,000 points and tier three for rewards worth more than 20,000 points. The benefit of a tiered structure is to motivate customers to stretch themselves to reach higher levels.

Upselling ratio: The number of purchases that customers make above and beyond the initial product they set out to buy in order to acquire more reward points.

Value-added proposition: Managing and enhancing value to both the customer and retailer.

Value at risk customer: A high-value, high-yield customer with a high propensity to churn.

RESOURCES

Introduction

Keenan, M (2022) 'Global ecommerce explained: stats and trends to watch'. URL: shopify.co.uk/enterprise/global-ecommerce-statistics

Casemine (2000) Royal Bank of Scotland v Wallace International Ltd. URL: www.casemine.com/judgement/uk/5a8ff8cc60d03e7f57ecd94b

Chapter 1

Castaldo, S & Mauri, C (1994) 'Supermarket customer loyalty promotions: an empirical study'. EGEA.

Crockett, Z (2019) 'The worst sales promotion in history'. URL: thehustle.co/the-worst-sales-promotion-in-history

Humby, C, Hunt, T & Philips T (2003) *Scoring Points: How Tesco is winning customer loyalty*. Kogan Page.

Hollie, P G (1984) 'Big Mac's Olympic giveaway'. URL: nytimes.com/1984/08/10/business/advertising-big-mac-s-olympic-giveaway.html

Cialdini, R B (1984, updated 2021) *Influence: The Psychology of Persuasion*. Harper Business.

Leahy, T (2012) *Management in Ten Words*. Random House Business.

Chapter 2

Ruzicka, A (2021) 'Shoppers shun supermarkets in favour of "top up" buys: Kantar'. URL: capital.com/shoppers-shun-supermarkets-in-favour-of-top-up-buys-kantar

Mercatus (2020) 'The evolution of the grocery customer'. URL: info.mercatus.com/egrocery-shopper-behavior-report

Gray, A & Lee, D (2021) 'Walmart vs Amazon: the battle to dominate grocery'. URL: ft.com/content/9ab41b9e-a294-430f-951d-49cfc3415460

UNCTAD (2021) 'Global e-commerce jumps to $26.7 trillion, Covid-19 boosts online sales'. URL: unctad.org/news/global-e-commerce-jumps-267-trillion-covid-19-boosts-online-sales

McKinsey (2021) 'US consumer behaviors and sentiment during the coronavirus crisis'. URL: mckinsey.com/business-functions/marketing-and-sales/our-insights/survey-us-consumer-sentiment-during-the-coronavirus-crisis

Hawkins, G E (1979) *Building the Customer Specific Retail Enterprise*. Breezy Heights Publishing.

SmallBizGenius (2022) '30 essential customer retention and brand loyalty statistics'. URL: smallbizgenius.net/by-the-numbers/brand-loyalty-statistics

Gallo, A (2014) 'The value of keeping the right customers'. URL: hbr.org/2014/10/the-value-of-keeping-the-right-customers

Motista (2019) 'Leveraging the value of emotional connection for retailers'. URL: static1.squarespace.com/static/6273e357746bf970e1d4f2c9/t/62f718e0494abd7a0776c4ec/1660360929034/Leveraging+Emotional+Connection+for+Retailers_0.pdf

Rheingold Institute (nd) Shopper psychology studies conducted for TCC.

Tidey, W (2018) 'Acquisition vs retention: the importance of lifetime customer value'. URL: www.huify.com/blog/acquisition-vs-retention-customer-lifetime-value

Nielsen (2012) 'Global trust in advertising and brand messages'. URL: nielsen.com/insights/2012/global-trust-in-advertising-and-brand-messages-2

Chapter 3

888 Sport (2021) 'Football gold: why your old sticker collection could be worth a fortune'. URL: 888sport.com/blog/panini-football-stickers

Hajducky, D (2022) 'Pele rookie card becomes soccer's first $1 million card, sells for $1.33 million'. URL: espn.com/sports/soccer/story/_/id/33272568/pele-rookie-card-becomes-soccer-first-1-million-card-sells-133-million

Peng, S (2022) '50 most valuable baseball cards of all time'. URL: stadiumtalk.com/s/most-expensive-baseball-cards-985687df1bbe45c5

Spaid, B (2018) Exploring consumer collecting behavior: a conceptual model and research agenda. Marquette University. URL: epublications.marquette.edu/cgi/viewcontent.cgi?article=1277&context=market_fac

Caven, R (2021) 'Life in plastic: it's (still) fantastic, say Barbie collectors'. URL: ft.com/content/6c32f4fe-abfd-45f7-acee-e7130b3e1132?shareType=nongift

Ferguson R (2017) 'The power of the golden moment'. URL: thewisemarketer.com/customer-engagement/insights-power-golden-moment/

Chapter 4

Woolf, B P (1996) *Customer Specific Marketing: The new power in retailing*. Teal Books.

Chapter 5

Smith, R (1997) 'Banana economics: buy 942lb of fruit, give it away — and make £25 profit'. URL: independent.co.uk/news/banana-economics-buy-942lb-of-fruit-give-it-away-and-make-pounds-25-profit-1283219.html

Carluccio, J, Eizenman, O & Rothschild P (2021) 'Next in loyalty: eight levers to turn customers into fans'. URL: mckinsey.com/business-functions/marketing-and-sales/our-insights/next-in-loyalty-eight-levers-to-turn-customers-into-fans

Chapter 6

Morgan, B (2020) '50 stats that show the importance of good loyalty programs, even during a crisis'. URL: forbes.com/sites/blakemorgan/2020/05/07/50-stats-that-show-the-importance-of-good-loyalty-programs-even-during-a-crisis/?sh=4254c1452410

Chapter 7

Antavo (2022) 'Global customer loyalty report — it's time to take action'. URL: antavo.com/wp-content/uploads/2021/12/Global-Customer-Loyalty-Report-2022-by-Antavo.pdf?vgo_ee=pvgGNIftAGt36pKzux2aGS6pA24HJsCUw0HRJQmoYB8%3D

Carr, S (2021) 'How many ads do we see a day in 2022?' URL: ppcprotect.com/blog/strategy/how-many-ads-do-we-see-a-day

Starbucks (2021) 'Starbucks reports Q4 and full year fiscal 2021 results'. URL: stories.starbucks.com/press/2021/starbucks-reports-q4-and-full-year-fiscal-2021-results

Sight-X (2021) Independent research, July 2021.

Cook, S (2022) '30+ YouTube statistics and facts'. URL: comparitech.com/tv-streaming/youtube-statistics

Ceci, L (2023) 'Hours of video uploaded to YouTube every minute as of February 2022'. URL: statista.com/statistics/259477/hours-of-video-uploaded-to-youtube-every-minute

Spar SA (2021) Independent research conducted for TCC.

McConnell, M (2021) 'Is Gen Z the most profitable consumer group in the UK?' URL: dma.org.uk/article/is-gen-z-the-most-profitable-consumer-group-in-the-uk

Digital Marketing Institute (2021) '20 surprising influencer marketing statistics'. URL: digitalmarketinginstitute.com/blog/20-influencer-marketing-statistics-that-will-surprise-you

Chapter 8

KPMG (2019) 'The truth about customer loyalty'. URL: assets.kpmg/content/dam/kpmg/xx/pdf/2019/11/customer-loyalty-report.pdf

Franklin-Wallis, O (2019) 'Plastic recycling is a myth: what really happens to your rubbish'. URL: theguardian.com/environment/2019/aug/17/plastic-recycling-myth-what-really-happens-your-rubbish

Plackett, B (2020) 'Changing diets at scale'. URL: nature.com/articles/d41586-020-03450-7

Chapter 9

Capper, A (2021) 'People belong to communities, not brands: the lowdown on Sid Lee's 'The Belong Effect' Study'. URL: lbbonline.com/news/people-belong-to-communities-not-brands-the-lowdown-on-sid-lees-the-belong-effect-study

WHO (2021) 'Obesity and overweight: key facts'. URL: who.int/news-room/fact-sheets/detail/obesity-and-overweight

Win International (2020) 'Annual world survey shows that almost a quarter of people consider themselves unhealthy'. URL: winmr.com/annual-world-survey-shows-that-almost-a-quarter-of-people-consider-themselves-unhealthy/

Chapter 10

Charm, T, Coggins, B, et al (McKinsey & Company 2020) 'The great consumer shift: ten charts that show how US shopping behavior is changing'. URL: mckinsey.com/business-functions/marketing-and-sales/our-insights/the-great-consumer-shift-ten-charts-that-show-how-us-shopping-behavior-is-changing

United Nations (2021) 'Global e-commerce jumps to $26.7 trillion, fuelled by COVID-19'. URL: news.un.org/en/story/2021/05/1091182

Briedis, H, Kronschnabl, A, et al (2020) 'Adapting to the next normal in retail: the customer experience imperative'. URL: mckinsey.com/industries/retail/our-insights/adapting-to-the-next-normal-in-retail-the-customer-experience-imperative

Curry, D (2023) 'Food delivery app revenue and usage statistics (2023)'. URL: businessofapps.com/data/food-delivery-app-market

Easton, E (2022) 'Postcode checker: how has your High Street changed since 2020?'. URL: bbc.co.uk/news/uk-63799670

Shahbandeh, M (2022) 'Global health and wellness food market value 2020-2026'. URL: statista.com/statistics/502267/global-health-and-wellness-food-market-value

Oberlo (2022) 'Why do people shop online?'. URL: oberlo.co.uk/statistics/why-do-people-shop-online

Cuofano, G (2023) 'Is Amazon profitable? Amazon profitability 1994–2022'. URL: fourweekmba.com/is-amazon-profitable/

Mando-Connect (2022) 'What the British want from loyalty programmes 3.0'. URL: mando-connect.co.uk/what-the-british-want-from-loyalty-programmes-3

AM Online (2023) 'Drivvn to sell £1bn worth of cars online in 2023'. URL: am-online.com/news/digital-marketing/2023/02/13/drivvn-to-sell-1bn-worth-of-cars-online-in-2023

Further reading

Keiningham, L, Vavra, T, et al (2005) *Loyalty Myths: Hyped strategies that will put you out of business – and proven tactics that really work*. John Wiley & Sons.

Lindstrom, M (2016) *Small Data: The tiny clues that uncover huge trends*. John Murray Press.

Mason, T & Knights, M (2019) *Omnichannel Retail: How to build winning stores in a digital world*. Kogan Page.

Price, M (2017) *Fairness for All: Unlocking the power of employee engagement*. Stour Publishing.

Reichheld, F & Markey, R (2011) *The Ultimate Question 2.0: How net promoter companies thrive in a customer-driven world*. Harvard Business Review Press.

Scammell-Katz, S (2014) *The Art of Shopping: How we shop and why we buy*. Viva Books.

Underhill, P (2009) *Why We Buy: The science of shopping – updated and revised for the internet, the global consumer, and beyond*. Simon & Schuster.

Walker, R (2021) *The Green Grocer: One man's manifesto for corporate activism*. Dorling Kindersley.

Other useful websites

Customer loyalty: thewisemarketer.com

US food retail: morningnewsbeat.com

Global food retail: theconsumergoodsforum.com

Retail trends: kateancketill.com

Reward trends: smartbrief.com

UK food retail: thegrocer.co.uk

UK marketing: campaignlive.co.uk

Global performance marketing: performancemarketingworld.com

Global brand marketing: mmaglobal.com

Brand growth and analytics: kantar.com

ABOUT THE AUTHOR

Richard Beattie is the founder and chairman of TCC, one of the world's leading exponents of retail loyalty building programmes. He started his professional career at the UK's largest bookseller/newsagent, WH Smith, and was later instrumental in founding Beattie's Newsagents. He subsequently led the negotiations and sale of the family business to a leading national multiple.

Having arrived in Australia to work for what became Rupert Murdoch's News Corporation in 1978, Richard became immersed in the world of 'continuity' promotions. He was responsible for bringing continuities to Australia for the first time, and it was here that he co-founded Wallace International with US-based entrepreneur Dan Wallace and began laying the foundations for what is now widely known in the industry as 'best customer marketing'. New market successes soon followed in New Zealand, South Africa and Europe and in 1984 Richard returned to London to be at the helm of Wallace's expanding global office network.

In 1991, Richard founded The Continuity Company (TCC) and a decade later, with offices established throughout Europe and North America, he set his sights on developing the Asia market, moving to Hong Kong in 2002. Here he introduced continuity programmes to further significant new markets in China, Taiwan, Japan, Thailand, Malaysia and beyond.

Since its inception, TCC has partnered with many of the world's largest food retailers, successfully delivering increases in revenue and market share. Richard's infectious enthusiasm for retail continues to this day, and with a 45-year track record in the industry, he is uniquely qualified to share his insights and experience in this book.

Now a permanent resident of Hong Kong, Richard passionately believes that TCC should be a force for good in the world and supports many charities through the work of the TCC Foundation (see below).

ABOUT TCC

TCC (originally The Continuity Company) was founded in 1991 with a mission to transform the way in which retailers connect with their shoppers. Harnessing a wealth of historical data and insights into the key drivers of customer loyalty, TCC develops marketing campaigns that change shopper behaviour, delivering sustainable sales growth and enhanced brand equity.

Today, the company is active in more than 70 countries, employing 400 people in 34 offices across the world. It currently has an annual turnover of $400 million.

Loyalty is now estimated to be a $50 billion-plus global industry that stretches across retail, online, hospitality, leisure and beyond. TCC has grown to become the world's leading exponent of customer loyalty programmes within its own niche area of expertise – most notably within the world's major grocery retail, fast food and petroleum forecourt sectors. And loyalty extends across many other sectors too.

For further information, visit tccglobal.com

About the TCC Foundation

Set up in 2017, the TCC Foundation aims to create brighter beginnings for children around the world. Its mission is to support children's development in meaningful, measurable and innovative ways by funding three vital areas: supporting healthy eating with resources and education; protecting vulnerable children with global disaster relief; and tackling child hunger where resources are scarce. It also provides grants to other charities that deliver programmes in line with the foundation's values.

Key partners include Save the Children, Médecins Sans Frontières, Amnesty International, Action Aid, Age Concern, Action Against Hunger, Homes for Humanity and UNICEF.

For more information, visit tccfoundation.com (and see lesson 49).